The Soul Baby, the Trickster, and the Golden Buddha

Spiritual Edition

By
Michael Roland

The Soul Baby, the Trickster, and the Golden Buddha

Spiritual Edition

by
Michael Roland
edited
by Walter Starcke
2014 © by Michael Roland
2nd Edition
Publication Date 31 October 2014
ISBN-13: 978-0983230311 (William Rayne Publishing)
ISBN-10: 0983230315

Country of Publication United States

Acknowledgements

First and foremost, I must thank Walter Starcke, MBA, L.Ac. Without his tireless effort this book would be nothing more than a string of idle ramblings lost in some forgotten sector of an abandoned hard drive. Thank you Walt. To Bunnie, who has been amazingly supportive; to Dr. Andrew Weil, Marilyn and Brad Browning, Christopher Sieveking, Philip Dutton, David McCormick, and to my mom Sharon who have read and offered much needed advice, criticism and encouragement; to my patients and clients who have taught me more than any; and of course, to my teachers who have generously and patiently helped me to build a foundation from which to learn and grow, I offer my humblest thanks. Thank you.

I would like to say a special thank you to some of the real-life individuals in this book who have allowed their names to be published within these pages. Dr. Evan Kligman, Dr. Jennifer Cato, Dr. Malcolm Riley, Master Liao Waysun, Curt Harmon, Marilyn and Brad Browning, Bunnie Haney, my father Joe Harger, my brother Joe Harger Jr., and Walt Starcke.

With the exception of John of God and Dr. Fuda, all other characters named in the book are fictional, composites of people I have known or met, or creations from my own mind. I should also point out here that I have no affiliation with John of God or the Casa de Dom Ignaci

Preface to the *Spiritual Edition*

When I first wrote this book a couple of years ago, it was entitled Soulbaby: A Spiritual Odyssey.

After writing the book and getting feedback that it was a good read, even "a real page turner," I thought to myself, there must be more here than just a story of my own personal spiritual journey. So, I asked my spirit guides to help elucidate the deeper meaning carried within each of the chapters. They replied immediately.

Each chapter now carries a quote from a particular spirit guide at the beginning and a short commentary at the end. Also, somewhat out of character, they chose to give me their names, which is interesting, because in the past when I have asked for names, they have indicated that names are either irrelevant or that any name they would give me would not actually identify them in a meaningful way. Maybe they made an exception here to help people identify with the message, I cant really say. I was not given an explanation. However, with all of my, now many, interactions with spirit guides and higher level entities, one thing is clear.

The one purpose for our time here on Earth and for the kind interactions that some of these higher beings offer to us, is for our spiritual evolution. It's the only game in town. Everything we do either aids or hinders that singular purpose.

For readers who are interested, I will give a brief overview of the individual entities who kindly offered their insights on each chapter.

Rayne: Rayne is the first guide who came to me consciously

and directly. She is very much like something out of a fairytale. As

i

with all guide level entities, she presents gender specific. This was quite interesting to me in the beginning. I had always imagined that if there was anything like spirit guides, that they would be without gender, but that's not so.

Rayne is incredibly beautiful, with long blond hair, lovely flowing gowns, and resonates love and compassion to a very high degree. It may not be evident in her quotes here, but she usually speaks in garden and nature metaphors. She enjoys strolling in her garden while beaming light down on all of her charges.

William: Stark contrast to Rayne, although they work as a

team. William's last lifetime, as near as I can tell, was as a 19th century surgeon. He is stern, incisive, and extremely logical. This was another big surprise for me. Everything in spirit conforms to logic. Logic is a gift from spirit not a hindrance to intuition as some frame it.

William always presents in a suit and one of those ties that is tied more or less like a bow, but not a bow-tie, with a beard and haircut appropriate to a 19th century surgeon and scientist. Although he has a high degree of compassion, he is quite severe and not at all effusive. In his current role, he works mainly as a spirit guide and alchemist.

His alchemy, like all true alchemy, is specifically designed to aid spiritual development.

I Lin: I Lin is the oldest of the human guides to make an

offering here. More later on other than human guides. I Lin's last lifetime was at least a thousand years ago. He is a Chinese Daoist

Sage who has chosen to put off his further ascendence in order to help those of us not so far along the path.

He is extremely humorous, in fact, I'm not sure if the name he gave me was really I Lin or a play on words meaning "I am Lin." this was much funnier to him than it was to me. He is by far the most humble of all the guides presented here. Also, one of the strongest.

Rey: Rey popped in just to offer comments. Rey's main

message is, "Do not to be distracted by from your path while on your journey.

The Angel: I know I am treading on dangerous territory

in terms of how people view angels, but here goes. Angels are not former humans. They are another species-something totally different than us. They are also enormous, powerful, and potentially terrifying beings. If you are near a spiritual presence that is kind, compassionate, gentle and loving, it is most likely a spirit guide, not an angel.

Remember, among the actions attributed to angels, includes execution...185,000 people at a time in the case of the Assyrians. I'm not a bible scholar, but it does actually give a better representation of the power, might, and and terrifying potential of angels.

I will leave this discussion to a later time, because I know it flies in the face of the current angel craze and I have no reason to engage in that debate. However, suffice it to say that angels are not and never were humans, and they are enormously powerful entities (that most of us have no reason to worry about).

This angel, I just happened to meet in the course of working with clients. It was a terrifying and physically painful experience. Although he meant no harm, his presence was so strong that the intensity of his vibrations caused my physical body to have pain just being in his vicinity.

I am enormously grateful to these beings for offering their insights and commentary in this book. All spirit guides are here to help us. It is a purpose that they have taken on out of compassion. We all have these guides and none of us are ever alone. They never give up and they will never leave us.

Introduction

Psychics are popularly thought of as people who predict the future or delve into past lives. Maybe that's why I don't consider myself a psychic, but more of an assistant at the spiritual level. My background comes from Chinese medicine and some ancient and esoteric studies commonly referred to as qigong. The core of my work is to help relieve people from their suffering and to assist them with spiritual growth whether in this life or the next. As spirits, it is our purpose to ascend and grow. To do that, we each need to make the most of this brief, condensed, physical experience that we call our life. It's a wonderful opportunity to expand ourselves into the universe. We need to make the most of every chance to learn our life lessons and to grow through experience, to unburden ourselves from ego attachments, and to evolve as authentic beings. Our existence is long, but this lifetime is short. We must remove our blockages and evolve as our true selves. This is the real purpose of my work and it's what's in the back of my mind each time I begin a telephone session.

"Hello, this is Jennie."

Jennie's first baby is ten days late. She is a doctor, educated, intelligent, and sincere. A friend of mine. I met her a few years ago when I was working at the University of Arizona. Her email said she is worried that she will have to undergo chemically induced labor instead of the natural birth she had hoped for. She asked me to to consult with her from five thousand miles away. What can I do?

I spend a few minutes, sometimes a few hours waiting for the arrival of the heightened state of awareness and spiritual connection that I need for my work. Even though it always comes,

I can never feel sure that it always will. I don't take it for granted that I will have the assistance required for my work. I close my eyes.

Mist clears. A colorless light beyond mortal vision unfolds from the murky shadows. Strength, compassion, and acceptance infuse the senses. Alignment of energies has been prepared and there is calm where there was anxiety. A consciousness greater than my own infuses itself into mine. The connection is open.

I am truly grateful for the opportunities I have had to help others and I am thankful that there are elevated spirits who have our best interests in mind. With a new calm, I begin.

"Hi Jennie, it's Michael."

"I'm so glad you were able to see me." "It's been a long time. How are you?"

"I'm pregnant and past due by ten days, and am facing hospitalization and drug-induced labor or a C-section, which I really want to avoid."

"OK, let's have a look."

Eyes, closed. Getting closer. Oh, there you are. Gosh, you're big and bright, and strong.

"Jennie, do you know the baby's gender?"

"We decided not to know, but I'm sure it's a girl."

"I see, well you could be right, but the figure I am looking at right now is definitely male. He's very bright and very strong. Let's stay with it for a few minutes and see what happens."

Excitement. He wants to come into his new incarnation, his new life, all the new experiences, learning and growing, he can hardly wait. This must be the baby. If he wants to be born, why is he ten days late?

"Just give me a minute Jennie."

"OK."

He's strong, he's happy, he's excited. He's not budging. What's going on? He seems very satisfied as if his incarnation is a fait accompli, but it's not. He must know that he still has to be born. His energy surges. Oh, I see. It's very difficult to compress a big spirit into a tiny physical body? It's frightening and takes a huge effort? I see. You would rather be born with a C-section? OK, I get it.

"Jennie, this may sound a bit weird..." "Yes?"
"He wants to be born via C-section."

"What! I thought babies all wanted natural births. Michael, I'm a OB physician and I can't see any reason why a C-section would be preferable from the point of view of the baby.

My midwife thinks I am holding onto to him and don't want to let go."

"Yes, I understand. Let me look into it a little further."

A crush of fear and darkness. It's like he is showing me a movie of his own big, bright spirit being crushed and stuffed through its life portal into this new incarnation – like being pushed through a funnel and down a roller coaster at the same time.

"It's very difficult for a big spirit like his to condense down into the physical. It hurts. He thinks if he gets the C-section, he won't have to go through pain of becoming physical again, but I don't know if he is right about that. The strange thing is that he is very excited about his new life. He's raring to go."

"Are you saying it's not my fault?"

"It's not your fault, Jennie. It looks like it's the baby who is holding back, not you."

Oh, I get it. You don't want to work for it, do you? You want the reward, but you don't want to put in the effort. That's it, isn't it? His whole energy pattern unravels briefly, past lives of reward without work, lacking the understanding of the value of making an effort. Ah, I see. This is one of the life lessons you have signed up for in this incarnation, isn't it? You're not even born yet, and you're already trying to get out of the work!

"Jennie, it appears that this is one of his life lessons. He has come here to be with you and to learn the value of making an effort in life – not just the value of the reward, but the value of the effort itself, something you might want to remember for the future. It's his big lesson for this lifetime, and he's already trying to get out of it. But don't worry, he is a big, bright, happy spirit otherwise.

As I am telling you this stuff about his life lessons and his already trying to get out of them, he seems to be listening. There's definitely a shift in his energy. I don't know if it will be enough to get him to engage in a natural birth or not. You'll have to let me know."

"OK. Thanks Michael."

"Hang in there Jennie, I hope to hear from you soon." "OK, bye."
"Bye"

*

Deep breath. Press the call button.

"Hi Sarah, this is Michael."

"Oh, hi. I found your website. I was hoping you could help me."

"OK. Tell me what is going on."

"I'm sad. All the time. I've always been sad. It's not like I'm sad, but there is always sadness around me. I don't know how to explain it. There's no reason for it. I had a great childhood. I'm successful. I've got a great husband. I'm just carrying this terrible sadness and I don't know what to do about it."

"Have you been to doctors or therapists?"

"Yes. I even spent six months in therapy. You know there is always stuff, but my therapist didn't think I was depressed. In fact, I'm happy! I'm just sad, too. I know I sound like an idiot."

"No, not at all. Let me tune into your energy and see what we can find. So, you've read my website and your comfortable with the work I do?"

"Yes."

"OK. Give me just a few minutes here. Oh, that's interesting."

"What?"

"You've got a huge crowd around you. They're all pushing in. It's a bit confusing. Just a minute."

Chaos, confusion, fear, desperation, smoke, water, fire, ice, a man lecturing at a podium, girls in old-fashioned dresses, somebody shoveling, 1840...a wreck.

"Wow, there is a lot going on here. This may take a while."

"Take your time. It's been thirty-five years for me."

It's been a great deal longer for them. All these different energies crowding in, I've got to separate them. Just slow down, everybody. I promise we'll get to all of you, but I can only do it one at a time.

A man, skin black sweaty and shining. Fear. Fire. Panic. OK, hold on, just stay with me. Good. You're OK. Stay with me. I'm going to help you. A portal of light opens, his fear is relieved. I can lift him. Up he goes.

"I think I've got things figured out here. I don't know why you might be associated with this, but I think I know what is going on."

"What? Tell me."

"It looks like there was a big train wreck or maybe a steam ship disaster and for some reason the spirits of the people who lost their lives and weren't able to cross over are attached to you. I don't know why. Does this sound completely strange to you?"

"Somehow it doesn't, it should, but it doesn't. What can I do about it?"

"There may be something for you to do, I don't know yet. For right now, the first thing we need to do is to free these spirits so they can get going on their way and get on with whatever it is they should be doing and stop hanging around you."

"How do we do that?"

"That's my job, but I may need some help. For now, do me a favor – close your eyes, and calm your mind. If you start thinking of something then just let it pass. Relax."

"I can do that."

"Good."

OK, who's next? Girls in dresses. I can send them easily. They have a welcoming committee waiting. Man in suit, doctor or professor, very serious. Up he goes. Dozens of people, one after the other, up they go. Exhausting.

"How are you doing, Sarah?"

"I'm alright. I feel kind of light-headed."

"I think you'll be lighter in a lot of ways. This is a heavy burden you've been carrying."

"Why me?"

"I'm not sure, but now that they're all gone, it will be interesting to see what happens with feelings of sadness. How do you feel now?"

"I feel great!" "Great!"

*

The whole shipwreck thing with Sarah was very intense. I wondered if it was recorded anywhere. So, I searched Google for "steam boat disaster 1840." It brought up this terrible tragedy:

The Republican Standard
Bridgeport, Tuesday Evening, Jan. 11, 1840

APPALLING CALAMITY
STEAMBOAT LEXINGTON DESTROYED BY FIRE, AND
NEARLY TWO HUNDRED LIVES LOST.

The day after our session, Dr. Jennie had a healthy baby boy by natural birth. She sent this email:

From: Jennie
Subject: Our Session
Date: July 4, 2010 3:15:36 AM To: Michael

Hi Michael,

Great news - I went into labor yesterday afternoon after our session, and we had a baby boy at home this AM, no C-section! I had been so sure it was a girl until we talked!

Thank you so much helping make that shift possible. First life lesson accomplished! :)

Jennie

PS: When I met you years ago, you were a clinician. Sometime when I'm not sleep deprived I'd like to hear about how you started on this new path...

How did I start on this path? I'm not sure how it began, actually. I wasn't born with any of these abilities. There was certainly nothing special about me as a child. And, there's nothing special about me now, really. In fact, none of this started until I was thirty-something, after moving to Tucson, Arizona.

Crystal Crisis

Quote from Spirit

"From turmoil and distress your journey begins to unfold. Out of chaos comes order. Your eyes begin to open, but you do not know how to see. Listen to your heart and put away your doubt. Lend confidence to your senses. Eschew fantasy and embrace the divine sight which is offered to you."
~Rayne

Glowing embers smolder in the southwestern sky as the desert floor sends its fire up to heaven. What is dying tonight will seek new life in the morning. The never-ending cycle of death and rebirth is clear for all to see. But to be a good witness you have to have your eyes open. I've still got my blinders on as I struggle with my head down, turning circles within circles. Car, house, job, debt, life.

It's a gorgeous day today in the Sonoran desert, clear and mild. I love feeling the wind when I drive. Stereo up and top down. I do my best to dodge the blue-hairs driving their Oldsmobiles with Nebraska plates slow in the fast lane. In the '70's Grant Road off I-10 was called the "ugliest street in America" by Life magazine. It hasn't changed much since then. It gets better by the time you hit Campbell Avenue. That's where my house is. Well, it was my house. I sold it to my best friend, Charles, with the agreement that I would rent it back from him. It worked out for both of us, but now I'm about to get kicked out of what was my own home.

It's a gentle kick. Really more of an I've been thinking about things and I've made some plans that don't coincide with you staying here much longer kind of kick. Luckily, he's given me some time to find another place. In fact, that's what I'm doing right now. I'm just on my way back from my new condo to be. My two-bedroom honeymoon cottage with French doors to the garden is no longer mine. Neither is my wife. We were divorced some months ago. My wife left amicably. Charles asked me to move amicably. Everyone seems to be feeling amicable except me. I don't feel much of anything. I'm somehow disconnected and set apart from it all, like I'm watching a movie dramatization of my own life. I pull into my side of the carport. Charles parks on the other side, nearest the gate. It is his house after all.

My new place is a little north of here closer to the foothills, but still in the same zip code. There's just something about living in 85718 that is that much more appealing than living in 85719. Bigger houses, nicer cars. At least, in the new place I've got high ceilings and an open floor plan. I've got no money, but great credit, testimony to having carried a huge amount of debt on my Visa and having adequately fed the financial machine for several years in succession. I am the proud owner of 3 percent of a new home; the other 97 percent is shared unequally between Countrywide Mortgage and Bank of America. After some new tile and a few repairs it will be ready to move into.

I've got to write. I am supposed to develop a module in an educational program that will explain Chinese medicine to medical doctors in sort of a Readers Digest format. Give them the basic idea, but don't confuse anyone. The educational program that I'm working on is being developed by my English friend, Malcolm, who works at the university. Happy, cheery, single and always surrounded by women, I don't know how he does it. Oh, well. I start slogging through the material. Type, type, type. I need to get the first section done so I don't have to feel totally stressed out and panicked about my deadline when I go to the exhibition this afternoon. You never know what strange and unique artifacts you might find at the Tucson Gem Show.

*

2

Rock hounds, fossil merchants and bone peddlers. There is an invisible underworld of eccentrics who dig the earth for hidden treasures. Its inhabitants come out of their secret places to meet once a year at the Tucson Gem and Mineral Show, the biggest show of its kind on the planet. Business is done at the largest conference centers in the city. Artifacts are traded privately in hotel rooms, and contraband is shifted on the side of the highway. For some, this is their biggest money-making event of the year. Thousands of tons of minerals, crystals, fossils, and meteorites land in Tucson, Arizona, in February of each year.

Walking around the courtyard of the Plaza Hotel on Old Main Street, I am overwhelmed by the variety of offerings. Dozens of hotel rooms open to the center plaza, each with its display of goods and each with its guardian at the door. Having travelled for days to get here, one of the gatekeepers sleeps on his bed next to hundreds of fossilized trilobites that have been meticulously laser-carved from their ancient tombs. Another stands at a slant in his doorway, with his left shoulder propping up the wall, dark circles cradling weary eyes that sluggishly sweep the courtyard for prospective buyers. He's in from Down Under and the jet lag is killing him, he says, as I pause near his doorway.

In the corner of the courtyard farthest away from the main exhibit, I spot a table full of crystals of different colors, shapes, and sizes. Their guardian, a dark Brazilian with bright eyes, watches over his offerings. It wouldn't matter to him whether he was selling rare birds poached from the Amazon or hand-carved wooden spoons. Each item has a price, and he'll decide what it is after a quick assessment of the keenness of your interest and the number of bills in your wallet. He correctly assesses that I have neither in great abundance. I buy a purple amethyst, about the size of my fist. It does not sparkle in the light as much as its comrades, but it seems heavier and denser. Ten bucks. It would get forty in a boutique anywhere else. My new acquisition rides home in the passenger's seat.

Ah, yes – home. My new condo. Two-car garage, high ceilings, and big windows – I'm moving up in the world. Still in the same zip code, but it's definitely a step up. The new tiles are in – big ones, not small ones. Twelve-inch tiles are no longer the in thing; they've got to be fifteen-inch to give the appearance of grandeur. Too bad I don't have money for furniture. I shouldn't worry too much about it, as paying the mortgage is the real problem. Luckily, I can set up my acupuncture office in the den and spare bedroom rather than renting commercial space. With a Japanese Shoji screen at the entrance to block off the living room, patients can come straight from the front door into my waiting room, bathroom, and treatment room area. This offers a nice, comfortable environment for my patients. But the house is not zoned for office space – the homeowners association wouldn't approve if they caught wind of it. I am quietly terrified of being found out.

Not having any money makes decorating a snap. Kitchen stuff I brought from the old house. Living room furniture, zero. Television, none. Dining-room table and office furniture are courtesy of what's left of the credit card.

Today I learned that most amethysts come from mines in Minas Gerais, Brazil. This particular one fills the palm of my hand and has a flat base with six facets that come to a point at the top. It weighs heavily in my palm as I gaze into its depths. I pass it from hand to hand, turning it over with each passing. I imagine that I can feel warmth coming from it when I cup both hands around it. Searching for the right spot, I finally place it carefully on the table in the corner of the waiting room and then stand back to look at it.

Tucson is full of woowoo people who believe crystals have special powers: to heal, to teach, to store energy or amplify it. I'm skeptical, but maybe I shouldn't judge too harshly, because, for heaven's sake, I am an acupuncturist. That's kooky enough to some people. I pick the crystal up again and hold it in my hand. Then I close my eyes and let my body relax as I concentrate on the dark, translucent mineral in my palm. I wait for some metaphysical occurrence, but nothing happens, so I put it back on the table.

Upstairs, I sink into my comfy bed for a quick Sunday afternoon snooze, but my head is full of the strange sights I saw at the mineral show. The one that keeps bugging me is the skull-and-bones salesman, a dark, little man with black eyes and black hair. His cramped apartment was stuffed with human remains. All clean, bleached, and boiled – and legal of course, but creepy. Small skull $500, large skull $1000. What was the difference? The small one came from an undernourished Indian woman who pre-sold her skeleton so she could feed her family. Her life expectancy was only 35 years so they didn't have to wait long for their money. The large ones must have been sourced from somewhere else. I didn't ask.

Feeling drawn to play with my new crystal again, I rouse myself and head down to my den-slash-waiting-room. I like the soft and cool feeling of the carpet between my toes as I tromp down stairs before transitioning onto the cold, hard tiles. I grab the amethyst off the table and head back up stairs. This time, rather than trying to sleep, I lie flat on my back and place the amethyst on my forehead between my eyes. My third eye, right? I close my eyes and feel the weight of the stone on my forehead. Its coolness is comforting. As I drift, my thoughts float and change – pictures of the day's events, pictures of friends, pictures of the desert are shuffling through my mind. As I continue to drift, I reach that halfway state between sleep and wakefulness. Now, that's strange... a shift in perception. What happened? I can see my chiropractor friend, Oswald. He is lost in the desert. I am seeing him through the stone, as if my mind is an eye and the crystal is a camera lens. He is standing in a barren desert with nothing around him but shifting sands. He doesn't know which way to turn. It must be a metaphor of some kind. I move on, and look at several of my friends in turn, one after the other. They each appear in sequence along with a sense of an associated emotion; lost, frightened, anxious, content. None of this is coming from my mind. It's coming into my mind – through the crystal into my mind. What the?! I take the crystal off my forehead and sit up on the edge of the bed rubbing my eyes. That's weird. Was that really happening, or was I just imagining it? A rumbling in my stomach tells me it's lunch time.

From the kitchen, I can see across the living room and up to the landing on the upper floor. The landing has a railing across the short hallway where the stairs end at the top. Whoa! I jump with a start. A young man is standing there with his elbows on the railing, his arms crossed in front of him with a beer can gripped slackly in his right hand. He is leering, and his face is twisted into a contemptuous grin. He looks like a B-movie version of a frat-boy-gone-bad. Except for one thing; he is not really there, at least not in the flesh. I see him in my field of vision while I look at the landing, but at the same time I know he is not physically there – it's like – seeing a ghost. Not only that, but I feel fear and tension in my body as if he had just made some rude comment or threatening gesture toward me. As I keep looking in his direction, his apparition remains. I'm going to stop looking. This is too freaky.

The doorbell rings. A tall, blond Nebraska farm girl is standing in my front doorway, Oswald's wife. "Hey, Sherri, what's up? Come on in." I've always known Sherri was psychically sensitive. This is an interesting time for her to show up for no reason.

"Hey, what brings you here?"

"I was just in this part of town and thought I would stop by to see how the move-in is coming along."

"Cool."

"Where did you get the couch?"

"Malcolm loaned it to me. Have a seat. Do you want anything to drink?"

"No. I'm good."

"I was just experimenting with a crystal I bought."

"Yeah?"

"I put it over my third eye and had these wierd visions. Do you want me to look at anything for you?" I lie down on the tile floor and put the crystal on my forehead. In the normal world this would be considered bizarre, but for Sherri it seems perfectly reasonable.

"Yeah, you can look at some protection amulets a shaman gave us in Bali. I don't know if they are still working."

I always try to keep an open mind no matter how ridiculous something seems. I wonder how much she paid for them? As I look into my crystal, I don't see the amulets; I see the shaman! He is very charming, charismatic, and smiling – not the intense witch doctor I had imagined when they told me about him some months ago. "Oh, that's interesting."

"What?" she asks.

"Was the shaman sort of charming and charismatic?"

"Yeah, why?"

"Because I see him, not the amulets. Where are they?"

"They're in our house." I try to look through the crystal into the house, but cannot find the amulets.

"Where in the house?"

"Mine's on the nightstand and Oswald's is in the dresser."

I think about the amulet on the nightstand in their bedroom and then I can see it, but it just looks like a pouch containing nothing but dry dust. "Uh, well, I don't think yours is working anymore. It looks dry and lifeless."

"I didn't think so. What about Oswald's? He quit wearing his when I thought mine stopped working."

I think about Oswald's charm in the dresser then I see a small packet, but instead of dry dust, I see a small vortex of swirling colors. Then I see the shaman again. He is smiling.

"Uh, I think his is still working."

Suddenly I feel a creepy sensation, and my body starts to cringe. I look at Sherri. Her face has gone pale, her head is nodding slightly, and her right hand is motioning as if she is trying to wave a fly away from her face. But there is no fly.

"Are you OK?" I ask.

"Yeah, you've got someone here." "No, just me and you."

"No. He's up there." She points, without looking up, to the stair landing where I saw the frat boy a few minutes ago. "He's talking to me."

My skin goes cold and little hairs stand up on the back of my hands. "What's he saying?"

"I can't listen. It's not good. I've got to go."

"Are you OK?"

"Yeah, I've just got to go."

I get up. "Yeah, yeah, OK, um, I'll walk you out."

"No. I'm good. I just have to go. I'll talk to you later." Sherri gets up slowly. "I like the house," her voice trails. With heavy eyelids shielding vacant eyes, she slowly navigates to the door, smiles, and waves in my general direction. "Alright, see ya," she says.

"OK, bye." The door shuts.

This psychic vision stuff is moving fast, too fast. I know I'm not making it up, but what is really happening? Is this just a bunch of nonsense? If it is nonsense, then why did Sherri hear a voice coming from the same place on the stairwell where I saw the specter of the college boy? I didn't tell her about it. I didn't have time to tell anyone, I've only just seen him myself. And how did I know that the shaman, thousands of miles away in Bali, was charming and charismatic instead of intense and scary like I had always imagined him to be? It's possible that Sherri could have just agreed with anything I said about him, but that still doesn't explain how she knew about the ghost on the stairwell. I don't think I'm going insane, but this is starting to freak me out.

I've got to get my head back together. I have to have a coherent mind set to treat the five patients scheduled for tomorrow. Not exactly a thriving practice, but it will pay the mortgage. Right now, I feel thin and transparent like a film negative of myself. It seems like light travels right through me instead of being reflected back. I'm tired.

Commentary from Spirit

Each of us is given opportunities to open our spiritual eyes. With each opportunity comes our option to embrace the truth that we are offered or to close ourselves off from the gift that is given.

Let your mind become at ease with information you don't understand. Open your mind to possibilities you have not yet considered.

The calling to Spirit comes to everyone, but only those who listen with openness and awareness can receive the beneficence.

The Green Troll

Quote from Spirit

"To use force is not correct. To wait for opportunity is not correct. To find equilibrium and to maintain balance is correct. Do not try too hard. Do not settle for less than your potential."

~I Lin

I wake up feeling exhausted. New patient in 45 minutes. Quick shower, a couple of soft-boiled eggs, and I'm ready. She's a referral from Evan Kligman, a local MD I know from the university. He sends me his headache and migraine patients. When she arrives, I open the door and I'm immediately stunned. I am looking at a thirty- year-old woman with long, brown hair, average build, and, growing out of her right temple, a semi-translucent, oversized, green troll head with a bulbous nose.

"Hi. Please come in." I smile, trying not to look at the slimy creature bobbing up and down from the right side of her head. "Did you have any trouble getting here?"

"No. I drove right here," she replies.

"Great. I'll get you set up with a couple of intake forms, and then we can go to work."

This is a real problem. We didn't go over this in acupuncture school. How should I report this to the referring doctor? Thank you for the referral. Patient presented with calm demeanor and large green troll head growing out of right temporal region.

I finish the treatment without ever letting on that I am going completely insane. Now I need a referral, but I don't think I'm a case for the university shrinks. I remember there is a Native American medicine man who occasionally works with the education program at the university. I dial Malcolm.

"Malcolm, what is the name of that medicine man who works with the program?"

"I'm driving right now, I don't have his number. Let me give you the number of my friend Brenda. She has all his contact info. And he is a 'Cherokee White Priest,' not a medicine man"

"OK, thanks. Ciao for now."

I quickly hang up and dial Brenda's number. She is British, too, but her accent, different from Malcolm's, sounds more like M from James Bond. After I give her a brief explanation of my problem, she offers the contact information for Jessie Clearspring, who lives just outside of Tucson.

I dial the number for the White Priest and get the answering machine. A woman's voice answers. "Hello, this is the phone of Jessie Clearspring and Sylvia Deerheart. Leave your number. We will give you a call back if Spirit approves." Hmm, how does that work?

"Hi, I got your number from a friend. I have this little problem that she said you could help me with. Um, basically, I put a crystal on my head, and now I'm seeing ghosts. Please call me back if you think you can help. Thanks." I leave my number and hang up.

An hour later the phone rings.

"Hi, this is Sylvia Deerheart. Jessie said he would like to see you as soon as possible." I guess Spirit approved.

"Oh, yeah, great, thanks. How do I get there?"

"We're out past Picture Rocks." She gives directions and tells me I can come this afternoon.

"OK. I'll be there. How much will the visit cost?"

"Jessie does not charge a fee, but a donation is welcome." I hang up. I'd never make the mortgage on that strategy. After my last patient, I jump in the car and head for Picture Rocks, which is about a half- hour's drive from Tucson.

I take a winding road through the desert. Armies of giant saguaros stand silently on the hillsides where the curves begin. With each bend G-forces gently push me from side to side as the scenery goes whizzing by. I turn off the music so the throaty purr of the exhaust note can mingle with the ambient noise of the wind. It lulls me into a focused hypnotic state that is both calm and aware at the same time. Ten more minutes to the White Priest.

I turn onto a dirt road and drive up to a gate where a tall, thin man with sharp features and a long graying ponytail stands sentry just inside. I stop the car. His face remains blank as he looks me over. He stands fast with his weight equally distributed onto both feet, making no move to clear the pathway for my entrance. The fact that I have a confirmed appointment apparently doesn't play a part in his decision process. After a long moment he opens the gate. As I drive in he shifts his attention from me to my little roadster. When I get out, the old indian continues to look at the car. He studies it carefully, peering into the cockpit and then inspecting the wheels. After completing his assessment, he stands back away from the car and says, "I had a Triumph Spitfire," then he turns to walk into his home. I smile.

A huge medicine shield covers one wall opposite the kitchen entrance. It is made of the stretched and dried hide of an animal. The skin is attached to a circular frame made of thin branches of gnarled wood twisted and bound with rawhide strings. Among the shield's adornments include a tortoise shell and the full wing – complete with feathers – of some large bird. As I gaze at this creation, my body is physically repelled while at the same time my consciousness gets drawn closer. The inside of the house is rustic and homey. Various other smaller medicine shields grace the walls.

There is a pack of American Spirit tobacco sitting on the kitchen counter.

Sylvia introduces herself and tells me how Jessie works. We all three sit at the kitchen table. I then explain my problem to Jessie. After some brief scribbling on a yellow legal note pad he looks me in the eye.

"You messed around with things you don't understand. Now I have to fix you. You forced open your third eye before you were ready to see. Now I have to close it down to where it is supposed to be. Right now, it is stuck wide open like the aperture of a camera lens. It is letting in too much light, so you see more than you can comprehend. Your time will come, but it's not now. You will develop your abilities over time through effort and discipline, not by some trick with a crystal that will only put you in danger. Sit over here," he motions to a plain wooden stool placed smack in the middle of the kitchen floor.

As I take my seat on the stool, he produces an eagle feather from the table and starts to lightly brush and tap my body with it in different places including my forehead. I don't feel anything special. After about thirty seconds he stops. He takes a step back and gently sets the eagle feather on a wooden tray on the kitchen table, then disappears from the room. In a moment he returns holding a small leather pouch tied to a string. His slim fingers open the pouch and then search through various items on the wooden tray. He places a dried kernel of blue corn, a dime-sized bear carved out of turquoise, and a pinch of American Spirit tobacco into the pouch. He says, "Wear this around your neck," then leaves the room. This time he doesn't return. I say thank you and hand Sylvia a C-note from my back pocket, say goodbye and drive home. I am not sure what happened with all the feather tapping, but at least I don't see any apparitions for the moment. As the day passes, I find that I am no longer assaulted by strange images. I am back to normal, more or less.

Commentary from Spirit

For those seeking spiritual development, there is always temptation to gratify the ego. Rejoice at what you are offered, but do not try to fly too high too soon. Build your foundation like the pyramid, stable and solid. This way, when you reach to great heights you will never fall.

Joe's Son

Two hundred dollars in cash, a set of brass knuckles, a .32 pistol, a diamond ring and a diamond stickpin were found on the body. My grandfather, John Wesley was shot dead on the street outside the gambling hall that he owned. My dad, Joseph, was only three years old.

With a ninth-grade education and a vague wanderlust, my father left home at the age of fourteen. He moved to San Francisco with the grand dream of becoming a tugboat pilot. As it turns out, the call to the sea never came to fruition, but it did get him out to California, where he eventually met my mother. That's how I ended up being born on the West Coast.

Childhood experiences can range from horrific to fantastic. Mine were somewhere in that broad, nebulous, vague expanse between the two. I'm not complaining. Could have been worse. At least it was exciting having cowboy criminal brothers and a larger than life father who would throw a shot-glass of gasoline onto the fire to get it started, causing a huge booming bellow of flame to shoot out into the living room and make the front door rattle in its frame, or flip the dining room table over – plates, food and all – if he felt he needed to make a strong point.

To everyone's benefit, my parents split up when I was six. I went with my mom, and, after a misspent youth, I managed to get an education and attend Five Branches Chinese medicine college in Santa Cruz. License to practice in hand, I moved to Tucson, Arizona, to start my professional life. One divorce, two houses, and three cars later, here I am.

It's taken me a while to get comfortable with being a professional, being married, being divorced, buying houses, doing all the things normal people are supposed to do. I suppose it's more or less the same for all of us – less than perfect start, leading to a few faltering steps forward, blindly groping for the future, but we carry on, trying to shape our lives into something that looks very similar to how we imagine everyone else's life is, or should be anyway. So, I find myself in a new condo, in private practice, and working for the university part-time. Job, mortgage, car payment, credit card debt, divorce. I'm normal.

Today, I am treating a well-known healer from Sedona who has lots of problems stemming from injuries in a motorcycle crash. Three of his four limbs were torn off and then surgically reattached shortly after clearing up the little issue of him being dead on arrival at the hospital. Curt is an interesting guy, enormously sensitive and skilled in his work. He lies down on the treatment table and immediately goes into a light trance, letting me get to work without distraction.

After a few minutes of tuning into his body's energy, using the same type of hands on therapy and acupuncture modalities I have always used, I notice that Curt is twitching. Thankfully, I'm not seeing monsters anymore, since I met the White Priest, but I am still sensing things that I had not noticed before. Right now, there is a swirling energy in the room that I can very definitely feel and almost see. In fact, when I look with my eyes, it's as if I can feel the swirling energy through my visual senses. I don't see it per se; I feel it with my eyes, like an image in Braille. As I continue my work, Curt's breathing slows and he drops deeper into relaxation, but his muscles continue to jump without provocation. The swirling energy begins to calm and condense over his head, right in front of me as I work. At the same time, Curt's body spasms violently and then suddenly goes limp. The condensed energy pattern above his head then evaporates leaving Curt completely relaxed and seemingly unconscious. As usual when I do this kind of work, my mind has become empty of thoughts. But this time, the room is crowded with energy and my hands seem to move of their own volition. I realize that I am no longer guiding my own work, but rather the treatment is being guided from a consciousness other than my own. After the session, Curt steps into the waiting room where I am sitting. He immediately sits down in the wicker chair and starts talking and gesturing with his hands.

"First, an angel was floating around the room, then she came down and hovered over my head. I felt my body go real calm. Then some time went by, I don't know how much. There were about six guys standing around the treatment table – one on my left near my feet was a big Indian with a spear (Curt motions with his hands to show a man holding a spear perpendicular to the ground like a walking stick). At the end of the table there was a guy in a suit. He was standing there like this, with his hands stretched out over me (Curt puts both hands out in front of himself at about chest level, palms down, fingers spread, one in front of the other). He said, 'Don't worry, Joe's son will take care of you,' It was cool. I feel great. Thanks."

"Yeah, nothing to it. Charles and I are going rock climbing on Saturday, maybe we can come up and see you on Sunday if you're feeling good."

"OK, we'll see you up there. You're going to love the new house!" Curt says.

"Alright, sounds good, we'll see you later, Curt." Curt leaves and I sit back down in the waiting room to think.

What was that? Another hallucination confirmed not to be a hallucination? Was it just some weird coincidence that I felt swirling energy in the room that condensed over his head, and that he saw the image of an angel floating around the room that came to hover over his face? "Joe's son will take care of you"? He doesn't know my dad's name! Who was the big Indian? Is it all just some strange chance that Curt would come up with this story?

Each patient I see now has something about them that I have never sensed before, a light inside their body, a feeling of electricity in their skin, or an aura of energy that surrounds them. Each piece of information offers me insights, like pieces of a puzzle, none of them giving me the whole picture, but each one adding to my understanding.

I treat a lot of psychotherapists in my practice. I don't know why. Maybe they are just better at taking care of themselves than the rest of us. Max is a particularly hard-science type of psychologist. He has a Ph.D. in early childhood development and is up to date on all the latest research. I've been able to help him with his chronic sinus infections and asthma. Today, it is just maintenance. He is feeling pretty well and wants to stay that way.

As I do my usual acupuncture treatment on Max, I start to notice colors dropping in from the ceiling into Max's body. By now, I am getting relatively comfortable with these unexpected phenomena. First, a translucent, green light drops down into his groin area. At the very moment it touches him, he takes in a big involuntary breath and lets it out slowly. Glowing, translucent sheets of light like brief squalls of rain shoot down from the ceiling onto different parts of his body, one after another, from the bottom of his torso to the top of his head. Seven lights come down: first green, then blue, purple, red, orange, yellow, and, lastly, white at the top of his head. A swirling tornado of grey light about a foot high erupts from his chest then immediately disappears as a red glow travels into his heart. Max breathes a big sigh.

"How are you feeling, Max?"

"Great! Very relaxed." He doesn't seem to know that lights are dropping out of the ceiling into his body.

At the end of the day I have a strange exhaustion, deep, as if I have somehow emptied myself from the inside out. I sit on my borrowed couch and ponder the day's revelations. Still thinking about Curt's comment about 'Joe's son,' I call the Old Man. I talk to my dad about once a year or so, but it's getting more frequent as he gets older. His wife answers,

"Hi, Gerry, it's Michael, how are you?"

"Oh, shit, Michael! Your sister's kids are running amuck. There's no money coming in. Your dad is always out with the horses. Jimmy's in jail because he never paid his goddamn traffic tickets. Your dad is going to have to bail his sorry ass out again. That's gonna cost us! Oh, and they caught Joe, Jr. He's in prison in New Mexico for armed robbery and attempted murder."

"Is my dad there?"

"Yeah. Joe, it's Michael."

"Hi, Son, what a ya doin'?"

"Nothing, just thought I would give you a call. How's it going?"

"Oh, everything is good. Well, Gerry thinks it's all a goddamn disaster, but I don't know. It's alright."

Yep, that's my dad. Huge rocks can be falling out of the sky and giant cracks opening in the Earth's surface, yet everything is okay. Wow, prison, that's heavy duty. When I think about all the possible paths my life could have taken, it's a wonder I made it into my thirties. Thank God for my mother.

"I was wondering, how come grandpa got shot when you were little?"

"Well, my dad owned a gambling house in Oklahoma. He was fair and gave good odds, so he started taking customers away from the other houses. He had a bodyguard who was this big Indian – Comanche, I think – named Big Jack. Well, one day Big Jack went out of town to go to his mother's funeral. That's the day they shot dad, right outside his own gambling hall. They shot Big Jack some time later, too."

I say goodbye to my father. This is getting more and more interesting. Could the tall Indian with the spear have been Big Jack, my grandfather's body guard? Was the guy in the suit holding his hands out and saying, "Joe's son will take care of you," my long dead granddad? Have things like this been going on around me all the time, but my perception of reality has been so limited that I was only willing to see what was commonly agreed to be there? Are my eyes finally opening in the way they talk about in books on metaphysics and spirituality?

Commentary from Spirit

In life, you face trials. They often begin with your family, who's trials may have begun with their family. You must realize that you are a child of Heaven, as are your parents. You were placed in your family for specific purposes, but your growth is your own responsibility. Be thankful for your gifts of awakening.

Hunchback

Quote from Spirit

"When you find yourself one with all, this is the natural way of things. Death and rebirth cease to have meaning."
~I Lin

It's still dark when I wake up. My talk with my father is still going through my head. It was interesting to learn about Big Jack and my grandfather, but the whole situation of my brothers being in trouble and my dad seeming not to notice what a complete mess things are has left me feeling estranged, conflicted, and isolated. Is my life a total disaster too and I'm just not noticing it? I'm sure I moved away from my family out of some sense of self-preservation, but now I feel disconnected, not just from my family, but from everyone and everything. I am somehow apart from the whole instead of a part of the whole.

I shake off the gloom and wake myself up with some loosening and stretching exercises. I'm meeting Charles at seven to go rock climbing on Mount Lemmon. We're up early to take advantage of the empty road and get on the mountain while it is still cool. The Mount Lemmon highway is a great drive – no on ramps, no driveways, no crossroads – just 26 miles of twisty mountain tarmac. Charles is the perfect passenger. He trusts me completely. The bottom of the mountain is a long series of sweeping curves. Charles sits in the passenger seat perfectly calm with his eyes fixed on the next turn. We cut a cool groove up the mountain as desert scrub, oak woodlands, and Ponderosa Pines fly by on either side.

Shooting out of the last corner of the tight twisties between Seven Cataracts and Windy Point, I hit the brakes, down-shift to second, and pull off the road at mile marker thirteen. From here we can see the whole valley lying below us with its surrounding mountain ranges forming a distinctive boundary between Tucson and the rest of the Sonoran desert. It's a short hike to Hunchback Pinnacle, a gneiss granite spire that sticks straight up from the side of the mountain. The spire is not particularly tall by rock climber standards, but the mountainside falls away for hundreds of feet below it exposing one side to a steep drop. And at the corner of Hunchback Pinnacle projects Steve's Arête, a knife-edge rock formation, craggy, weather-beaten, and vertical.

We step into our harnesses and connect them to the climbing rope with figure-eight knots tied to the thick D rings looped through our harness belts. Charles ties into one end of the rope. I tie into the other. I stay on the ground and feed rope as Charles's long body begins the ascent. Gliding up the corner of Hunchback, he pauses momentarily every few meters to clip the rope into the permanent safety bolts that have been placed on the route, then continues his upward journey. Within a few short minutes Charles reaches the summit. He clips into the anchors and sets up a belay line to secure my climb.

Sweat greases my palms as I consider the rock face in front of me. Digging into the chalk bag attached to my belt, I dust my hands dry with the white powder. A long breath steadies my respiration. I reach as high as I can to make the first hold. Sharp edges of cool, gneiss granite dig into my fingertips as the weight of my body pulls hard stone into soft flesh. Jamming a toe into one of the sinews of Hunchback, I hoist myself onto the rock. One move at a time I creep up the craggy sport climbing route known as Steve's Arête. Stopping at the first bolt, I steady myself so I can handle the rope with one hand while my remaining appendages work to keep me attached to the rock. I unclip the rope that Charles had placed on his ascent. He clips, I unclip. That way we have the rope free when I get to the summit, so we can rappel down.

Midway, I look up at the arête. I can see it begin to arch out backward over my head. I look down. The mountain falls away hundreds of feet below me. I hear a loud, forced exhale. It's my own. It's the sound rock climbers make when they are trying to steady their nerves. From Charles up above, nothing. He knows this sound comes when someone is confronting his fear. It's a private matter. Charles quietly waits for me as I work out my issues with the rock. He understands that rock climbing is not so much a sport of strength and balance as it is a head game.

My right toe, jammed precariously into a small crevice, struggles to support my weight as the middle two fingers on my left hand dig into a thin lip of rock. I look for the next hold and see nothing but rough granite that eludes my grasp. Twisted and contorted, I desperately try to adhere to the stone. My pores open with sweat. I'm stuck motionless and my muscles are fatiguing. Within a few moments in this awkward position, my right leg begins to quiver involuntarily, jumping up and down hinging on the ankle. "Elvis" – that's what rock climbers call it. I tell my leg to stop it, but my leg doesn't listen. It keeps pumping like a mad seamstress on an antique Singer sewing machine. I cling desperately to the rock face instead of leaning back on straight arms to maximize my leverage. My quivering leg is going crazy. Hands wet with sweat try to grip granite from the wrong angles. Suddenly, my right leg bucks and throws me off Hunchback Pinnacle. I feel my heart move up to the position naturally occupied by my throat: I'm falling! In a pointless gesture I grab the belay line, which is already tied fast to the D-ring on my harness. Then I suddenly realize the rope won't hold. I can feel the line stretch to breaking point. My harness creeps up on either side of my groin as the full weight of my body plunges downward, surrendering to the irresistible pull of gravity. The rope will soon reach its maximum stretch: this is where it snaps and I fall to my death. But first I will suffer gory injuries with broken bones protruding through torn skin.

At the very end of the stretch in the rope, the point at which it will snap apart, the rope suddenly springs me back up and onto the rock.

My hands touch the cool granite and I scrabble for a hold, any hold. Finding one, I cling tightly to the granite surface, my heart beating furiously. I'm safe.

"You good?" from above.

"I'm good." I say in a loud and brawny voice, disguising abject terror.

That's how rock-climbing ropes work. They stretch so you don't hit the hard end of the rope with a dead stop, causing injury. They are tested and certified. I know this. Time to regroup and get it together.

Climbing upward, I reach the part of the route that leans backward over itself. I am relieved to find that the holds are big, deep, and positive – buckets. I sink half of my hand into one of the large buckets, lean back, and allow leverage to push my feet into the granite. It's a rush to hang out like this, arms straight, with my body leaning back off of the tower and nothing underneath but air and the valley below. Above the overhang there is only a round hump before the summit. There, the angle of the climb is no longer beyond vertical, but the buckets are gone, leaving only rounded mounds of coarse rock to palm. Friction climbing. Creepy. You plant a sweaty hand and pray that it sticks while you pull yourself over the hump. The summit is within a few feet. I stick to the rock, but my composure starts to slide away. Scrabbling and scraping with hands, feet, and knees, I make the summit and clip into the top of Hunchback.

I lie on my back and look up. Nothing but sky. Deep, long, slow breaths fill my lungs. With my heart beating in my eardrums, I close my eyes.

"Chips?" Charles asks.

Oh, yes. Sweet! Corn chips and a can of tuna fish. We munch in silence as we look out over the valley. With stone below and sky above, all thoughts fade as we continue to look out from our perch. We sit like Buddhist monks high on a mountain, all senses drifting away; all sense of self losing meaning as we fill the space between primeval earth and primordial heaven.

fffwwhhhTTTHHHHHHSSsshhh! A hawk flies just over our heads, the wind quietly shouting past its wings, looking for something that doesn't want to be found. The hawk doesn't see us. We have melded into the stone. We now gaze quietly from its ancient eyes. We are not humans, not people. We are just part of nature.

If I had died in my fall just minutes ago, would I feel any different than this? Would I ascend into heaven? Would I still be me or would I meld anonymously into the void? A great sense of peace touches me and I suddenly realize that in this very moment, I am connected and integrated into my surroundings, yet at the same time, I remain myself. I am separate, yet part of the whole.

Commentary from Spirit

Fear is a natural mechanism of protection. In the moment, it can help to preserve your physical life so you can benefit from the spiritual growth that is the purpose of your existence here. It is valid.

Fear that is carried with you perpetually in your heart, blocks you from the spiritual growth that is before you. Give up fear and embrace spirituality. Without fear you can connect yourself to all of creation.

Midnight with Master Liao

Quote from Spirit

"So, now you see light where there was darkness. Do not be distracted by the manifestation. Seek only the Source."
~Rey

Flying backwards through the air, wondering when, where, and exactly how hard you are going to land is a singular experience. This is happening to me right now. Just before take-off I had been sitting in the audience of a tai chi seminar listening to Master Liao Waysun. He was explaining mind-over-matter and action-without-force, the sort of thing you hear New Agers pontificate about at organic coffee shops. I have to admit, I am partial to these concepts myself. That's what got me into acupuncture and Chinese medicine in the first place. But my experience helping patients with intractable pain and chronic illness has forced me to give up some of my earlier notions of mysticism in the face of doing things that actually work in the physical world. So, when I hear someone talk about moving a thousand pounds with one ounce of force, I say, "show me." That's exactly what I did with Master Liao, and that's how I ended up flying through the air like this.

The wall rushes to meet my back faster than I can move my arms to brace against the impact. A few moments later my senses catch up to me and I find my feet just in time to save my vanity. The sudden acceleration and hitting the wall didn't hurt so much as it surprised me. I might offer a more polite challenge to the next tai chi master I meet.

I went to this seminar because of Allen, an acupuncture colleague of mine. He is a Buddhist with a gentle, soft-spoken demeanor. A few weeks ago he told me about a tai chi seminar he was planning with Master Liao, his tai chi teacher for the past twenty-five years. I thought it sounded interesting so I signed up.

Liao Waysun is tall and thin with smooth, white skin. He is in his fifties, but he's one of those people whose appearance offers few clues about his age. His arms and chest are thin. Clothes hang loosely on his tall frame. There is no evidence of muscle anywhere on his body. Master Liao's movements are soft, graceful, and fluid.

The afternoon portion of the seminar is called "Push Hands." Push hands is a method for tai chi enthusiasts to test their skill on an opponent without hurting each other or, according to Liao, it is a method of building qi and sensitivity. Qi (chee) is the invisible energy that the Chinese philosophers believe to be the motive force behind all action and being. It's also what acupuncturists believe to be the underlying energy of the body. When qi is correct we are healthy. When it has a problem we are sick. To Master Liao qi is the basis of tai chi. He says, "You don't use your body in tai chi. You use your qi."

I find myself without a partner during the Push Hands seminar, so Master Liao invites me out onto the training floor to push hands with him. Pushing is a bit of misnomer. It's more like touching and following, a game of sensitivity. As soon as the back of my hand touches his, he yields to the light force. If I follow, I will be off balance. If I don't, I will be vulnerable to attack. He guides me to follow, slowly and gently. Then at the point of my maximum extension, he pushes back with the faintest force. I respond by yielding to his gentle push. Master Liao calls this building sensitivity and building qi, but it is an unpredictable game. As I push back with a force that is ever so slightly too clumsy, he yields to make an opening that I fall into. My weight shifts forward and then something happens, but I'm not sure what. It's like the blink of an eye; a momentary blip in concentration and my whole world is upset. Master Liao touches me on my body somewhere, the elbows and the shoulder I think, but the only thing I am sure of is that I am flying backwards again.

I can see Master Liao standing calmly with his hands pointing at me or rather through me as if he is guiding my flight with his fingers while I am desperately trying to keep my feet under my body so I don't end up on my head. The force of acceleration is magical, as if a gale force wind is taking me. It's more like I am being pulled backward in the direction of travel than being pushed from the front. I am moving with such speed and force that my arms trail like streamers. I hit the wall again before I can brace for the impact.

I peel myself off of the wall and continue training. After an hour of push hands, my legs are like limp noodles. Pathetic, but it's the same for the other students. Master Liao, in his fifties, doesn't show any form of strain or fatigue.

At dinner after the seminar Master Liao tells me about his friend in Taiwan who cures cancer with acupuncture. He claims Dr. Fuda treats two hundred patients a day. Normally I am skeptical about cancer cures, but after experiencing Liao's supernatural ability I have to wonder if his friend has skill that is beyond normal as well.

After dinner Master Liao and I return to my house, where we sit in the living room and relax with a cup of tea and talk. He grew up in Taiwan. From the age of eight until he was twenty, Liao studied tai chi in the Daoist temple near his home. His friend, Dr. Fuda, studied acupuncture at the Buddhist temple. Later, they went to university together. Dr. Fuda studied medicine and Master Liao studied ancient Chinese language.

After university, Master Liao's research into tai chi took him to the Imperial Libraries, in Beijing, where he discovered a treasure of writings alluding to the origins of tai chi. Interpreting ancient

Chinese texts takes a lot more than merely understanding what the words literally mean. The first Chinese characters were written eight thousand years ago, and the language has been changing and evolving continuously ever since. Many of these written characters have changed over time and have various layered meanings, so the cultural and political landscapes of the time must be understood. Complicating things even further, clever scribes sometimes concealed the true meaning of certain works by using the written characters' historical meanings rather than their currently-used meanings of the time. Finally, even a scholarly understanding of the language may be insufficient to decipher certain old Chinese texts. These require initiation into the subject at hand – in this case, tai chi.

According to Master Liao's investigations, tai chi was not conceived as a martial art. In fact, the man said to have discovered or created tai chi was not himself a martial artist. He was the scribe at White Cloud Temple in Beijing. At the age of seventy he retired and went to the mountains, where he studied with Daoist spiritual masters. Upon returning from the mountains he had no money and was forced to travel alone and unprotected across hostile territory. On his journey he met a group of bandits who had been eluding the Imperial Guard for an embarrassing stretch of time. When the bandits set upon the now-eighty-year-old man they got a big surprise. He defeated them with his bare hands. Liao tells me it wasn't martial genius that helped the old man beat his attackers, it was his connection with the Dao.

"Master Liao, how does being a Daoist help an old man combat experienced robbers?"

Liao smiles.

"Michael, remember today when I push you?" he asks.

"Yes."

"Did you feel me push or did you only feel yourself fly backward?"

"Well, I know you touched me, but I can't say that I actually felt you push me, not with the force it would take to throw me against the wall like that."

"Right, that's because I didn't push you," he says. I can't tell if he is smiling or not.

"What do you mean?" I ask, taking the bait. "Physical bodies respond to physical laws right?" "As far as I know, I can't argue with that."

"Laws of physics apply to physical bodies. Laws of physics also apply to qi-energy bodies. Only different laws." He takes a sip of his tea and looks at me with raised eyebrows and smiling lips – he can see little lights turning on inside my head.

"So when I push you, I didn't push your body. I gave you a message, a qi message. My qi talk to your qi. It said 'go back, now'," he gestures with both hands as if he were holding two pistols pointed at me.

"Your body had to follow because you cannot separate your qi from your body. You can't stop it. If you do, then qi and body separate. You die. Body has to have qi to be alive, so you go back."

I've heard this a million times in Chinese medicine school, but it never hit home like this. If he can give me a qi message that sends my body flying backward with massive acceleration, then that must be how acupuncture needles give qi messages to suggest how the body can heal. They are just different messages. In an attempt to conceal my sudden enlightenment, I smile and nod knowingly.

"How come you can do this but I can't?" I ask.

"Because I am closer to the Dao than you," he says. "Let me show you."

For the first time I notice that Liao isn't sitting on his chair the same way I am sitting on mine. His feet are spread slightly wider than mine and they are centered under his body. When he stands up

30

it is as if he was never actually sitting. It's more like he was squatting in space exactly where the chair had been. There is no shifting of weight, no bending or tipping of his body as he stands up, just an effortless levitation. I am as amazed by his elegant rising from the chair as I was by his explanation of the push-message. Master Liao moves to the center of my empty living room and motions for me to join him. Immediately I look for a good place to land.

"Don't worry, I don't push you now."

We assume the push hands position with the backs of our hands touching. I try to remember what I was taught this morning, to relax and settle my body and calm my mind. We begin the slow, gentle, back-and-forth motion of single-hand push, and then he begins to move more freely, outside of the set circular motion that we learned in the seminar. I follow.

"OK, now you push me," he says.

As I push toward his chest, I can feel myself begin to fall forward because I am expecting to push on him, but there is nothing there to push. He has somehow evaded me. I try again to push on his body, but again there is nothing there to push. Master Liao says, "The Dao is empty so I am empty. You cannot push me because there is nothing for you to push. Only emptiness."

We sit again.

"Master Liao, we studied Daoism a little in Chinese medicine school, but nobody could ever really explain what Daoism is," I say, hoping to stimulate another transmission.

"Daoism is only one thing – returning to the Mother. Daoist want to go to Dao. Christian want to go to God. Buddhist want to go to Emptiness. But, ultimately it is one. There are many heavens before you get there, many other places, but there is only one Dao. Only one ultimate God. Only one ultimate Emptiness. This is Dao," he says taking another sip of tea.

"So, what does tai chi have to do with Daoism?" I ask.

"You want to go to Dao. How do you get there?" he asks, obviously a rhetorical question. "Practice tai chi, moving meditation. Make your physical body and your qi body one, together in harmony. Make your qi and your spirit one then you can touch the Dao," he explains.

"If you can touch the Dao, then death has no meaning. You just walk into Dao." Master Liao gracefully extends his right hand forward, fingers up as if he is pushing through a gossamer curtain and closes his eyes. His body seems to elevate and expand at the same time.

He opens his eyes. "OK, it's getting late." That signals that the lesson is over and it's time to take him back to his hotel.

It's a warm and beautiful desert night. The streets are quiet. Master Liao could not look more out of place in my little sports car. He is sitting bolt upright with a placid expression. His long, thin legs lie at angles that don't match the unnatural aspects formed by the leather and plastic interior. His right hand rests palm up on his right knee. He says nothing nor does he look from side to side as we travel. When we arrive at his hotel he gets out.

"OK, you call me about Taiwan and Dr. Fuda."

He turns and walks away. For the first time I notice that he is very well dressed in slacks, white dress shirt, navy blue sports coat and wire-rim glasses. Anyone expecting their tai chi master to be wearing robes and sporting a bald head and grey chin beard will be disappointed when they meet Master Liao. That is, until they begin to understand the depth of knowledge and skill he possesses.

Commentary from Spirit

It is easy to be dazzled by something you have never seen before. Do not allow your mind to become fascinated by by a show of power, prowess, or mastery. Seek to understand the underlying connection to source energy that makes it possible.

Green Tea and Breadfruit

Quote from Spirit

My heart is as big as a mountain, yet I bow beneath your feet.
Tread on me. Through my lowness, I raise humanity.
~I Lin

Fifteen hours in the wing seats, L.A. to Tai Pei. Allen is sleeping soundly with his head against the cabin window. I am ready to climb the walls. My back aches. My neck hurts. My nerves are on edge. We're right next to the constant thunder of the engines and I haven't slept for 24 hours. In two more hours we land in Tai Pei, then we've got another flight to Kao Sheng. Tucson seems far, far away.

Finally, we touch down in Tai Pei and get off the plane. As Allen and I move through customs, I'm fascinated by how radically different cultures can have thoroughly identical customs agents. Bang, stamp, grimace. The excitement of being in a new country is enough to temporarily counter the crushing fatigue. After stretching our legs with a quick walk through the corridors of the Tai Pei airport, fifty-five minutes to Kao Sheng is a cinch. When we land, we get a taxi to the center of town.

The southern edge of Kao Sheng is a seaport, but the smell of rotten fish permeates the entire city center. The air is moist and warm. We've got a half a day plus a night's sleep to recover from jet lag before we meet Dr. Fuda. Allen and I dump our suitcases in the hotel and head out to take in the local ambience.

We leave the hotel and step out onto the streets of Kao Sheng in the mid afternoon. Heat wafts up from the pavement as we exit the Grand Hai Lai Hotel. The streets are packed with motor scooters.

34

The girls all wear nylon windbreakers backward so their clothes are fully protected from the front, presumably to keep the road grit and thick smog off their blouses. Scooters buzz by us – one, two, three, sometimes even families of five on one motor scooter. Baby in front, then dad, number two in the middle, then mom, oldest on back. The traffic flow suggests a vague semblance of order, like an ant trail or a school of fish. The whole colony moves with one organic consciousness changing and flowing with no outward signal. We weave our way through throngs of pedestrians, whizzing scooters, and honking cars. We become part of the flow.

In Kao Sheng every corner has a food monger, noodle merchants being the most common. We stop to inspect a street-corner vendor who has a rack full of white-bread sandwiches with the crusts cut off. Tuna, yellow corn, and garbanzo bean fillings are on the menu today. We pass on the sandwiches and continue along the street in search of something a little more ethnic. The street vendors begin to multiply as we get closer to the downtown market. We spot a busy tent with steaming pots reeking of exotic aromas. Inside the tent in the back the locals are huddled around makeshift tables, talking and eating. They all seem to have the same dish. Allen and I look at each other and nod in agreement.

"Two, please."

We get our message across with a combination of English, hand gestures, and Allen's slim knowledge of Taiwan Wa, the local dialect. The vendor, who looks amazingly Anglo, panics at our request. She shakes her head, smiles a nervous smile, and searches in vain for someone to bail her out of this confrontation with foreigners. We smile and make more hand gestures. Finally, she opens up one of the steaming pots and dips in a ladle. She fills two bowls with noodles, gelatin, and odd bits and hunks of some kind of organic matter, possibly pork. Nervously glancing from side to side, she tries to judge what impact the round eyes will have on her business as she hands us each our bowl of street vendor surprise.

The locals go silent and shift uneasily. We find an empty table and sit down on plastic chairs. I fish out a pair of clean-looking plastic chopsticks and a spoon from the container of well-worn plastic utensils on the table. Digging into my bowl I am able to capture various bits and pieces with my plastic sticks. The texture is soupy, slimy, gelatinous, and oddly crunchy, like cartilage from a well-cooked chicken leg. The taste is savory and sweet at the same time. It's an instant favorite with us. The locals stop staring after we take a few more bites. Tension and worry assuaged, the vendor releases us from her scrutiny as well. Smiles and nods all around, our humanness is judged to be adequate by the locals: we eat like them.

After paying a pittance for our snack, we head across the street to the market. The fetid scent of the Asian market is thick in our nostrils as we enter the covered bazaar. Chickens, MP3 players, laser beams, sides of beef, and hog jowls line the myriad tables and benches. Row after row of anything and everything, price negotiable. We are instantly spotted as tourists. "Hello-hello." Every English word comes in two's in Taiwan. Hello-hello, thankyou-thankyou, byebye-byebye. Mostly it's hello-hello over and over. Being obviously non-Asian, we are targets. Each merchant takes his best shot as we pass by. Travel fatigue begins to set in as we walk through the covered market. Shopping for hog jowls and pocket laser beams will have to wait until the fog in my head burns off. The hotel room beckons, so we weave our way back through the streets of Kao Sheng toward the Grand Hai Lai.

At the hotel, Allen and I find our respective beds and crash hard. Sleep rushes at me like a train. I can't stop it. It comes so fast that I am still conscious when it hits, deep blackness and heavy weariness, then nothing. Hours later I wake with a gasp as if my lungs have just been turned on again, the first pulse of respiration jolting me awake. The room is dark, but I can hear Allen stirring. Time is upside down. It's 11 PM in Taiwan, but in Tucson it's 8

AM, morning for us. We decide to take another look around downtown Kao Sheng.

The noodle shop windows are clouded with steam, and we're both starving. Stepping into a corner shop we run our eyes over a selection of dishes wrapped in plastic. They all look essentially the same, either a bowl of noodles in soup or a plate of something that vaguely looks like tofu bathed in red dye number two. We choose our poisons – noodles for me, red dye number two for Allen – and sit down to eat. The place is packed, mostly young people trying to have a night out without spending much money. The vibe is good and the people are animated. The boys are trying to impress the girls. The girls are chirping away to each other, pretending not to notice the boys. Pungent exhaust billows in from the street.

Warm and sticky with full tummies, we traverse the sidewalks of downtown Kao Sheng. Shiny suits on scooters whiz past with girls in skirts riding sidesaddle on back. A new variety of street hawker populates the sidewalks. These hustlers come in twos and threes; safety in numbers. Pale, translucent skin below their buzzed scalps suggests that they don't see much daylight. Blood-red betel nut juice, oozing out of the cracks between their teeth, makes them look scary and freakish. When not accosting wayfarers, they spew the gory red liquid out onto the sidewalks.

High on betel nut juice, two of the night creatures lie in wait for Allen and me, the whites of their eyes showing above their corneas. We turn the machismo up slightly several yards before our encounter. Striding confidently with smiles on our faces and hands at our sides, but palms facing slightly forward, we walk through the gauntlet. They are aggressive, but not intent on harming us. Hands on our shoulders, they try to stop us on the sidewalk. "Hello-hello, girls inside, you like" they say, blood-red juice dripping down their chins. I can feel Allen starting to simmer. We smile and wave them off as we push through their human barricade. They mutter obscenities in the local Taiwan Wa as we pass by. Block after block, the red-fanged night creatures try to drag us into their Karaoke dens. If they weren't so pushy, we would probably give it a try out of curiosity, but, as it is, we're not sure we would get out intact. So, we leave it.

Back at the hotel, we decide to have a drink before retiring. The bar is modern and stylish with plush burgundy carpeting and round, dark wooden tables each with four soft leather bucket seats. It's quiet except for a few businessmen at the bar and a table with two beautiful Asian women in evening gowns. Melted ice in their drinks tells me they have been nursing them for a while. Allen and I order drinks. Savoring the aroma of the warm cognac, a luxury at home, but affordable here, I sit comfortably, letting my body try to sort out which hemisphere it is in. One of the girls in gowns has crossed her legs and adjusted the hem of her dress for the third time. I point them out to Allen. They both smile as he looks over his shoulder at them. Allen assures me the girls in gowns are high-end call girls. Finishing our drinks, we smile at the girls and head up to our beds.

Allen hits the sack and is snoring within minutes. I lie here, wide-awake in my bed. My body is sure it's late morning and not time for sleeping. I toss and turn as my mind races with sights, sounds, and scents of this new land. Hours go by and I still can't sleep. I'm awake to hear Allen's clock go off as the sun comes up. He is going out to the park to practice push hands with the locals. I am crippled with fatigue. I try to get some sleep after Allen steps out, but it's not happening. A hot shower and shave offer some veneer of alertness. In the lobby I meet Master Liao. A few minutes later, Allen limps in slightly hunched over with a sheepish look on his face. He had an unfortunate push hands experience in the park. It looks like the landing didn't go so well.

Master Liao is dressed in expensive, light beige-colored slacks, and a white dress shirt. Allen and I, in jeans, Hawaiian shirts, and shabby baseball caps, look like slobs by comparison. Master Liao explains that Dr. Fuda treats two hundred patients per day in his private clinic; and he has no nurse, no assistant, no telephone, and no appointment book. Forty percent of his patients have or have had cancer. The first day we should just stay out of the way and let him work. We will have a chance to talk with him later at his home. In a few minutes the car will be ready to take us to Dr. Fuda's clinic, about ninety minutes away in the town of Ma Do.

Master Liao sits in the front seat with his right hand resting palm up on his right knee. His eyelids are half closed. Allen and I are in back with our noses glued to the windows, our eyes wide. Even the simplest dwelling grabs our attention. Houses are placed indiscriminately between light industrial areas. All the homes are built from one plan, the same one as the shops in the suburbs of Kao Sheng, three stories, all glass in front on the bottom, with tile floors and a staircase going up. Any number might be joined together side by side.

In Ma Do, the houses are close together and smaller than their more industrial-style counterparts we have seen from the road. This is a Daoist town. In fact, there is at least one temple on every street. House, house, temple, house, house, house, temple, and so on. Each temple is slightly smaller than the average house, open to the front and some having iron bars across the entrance. They are full of very detailed and ornate statues of gods and local deities. This is religious Daoism, not the transcendent Daoism of Master Liao.

Down a narrow lane lies Dr. Fuda's clinic. In front is a large tree encircled by a bench. Elderly people, some with bicycles nearby, have parked themselves on the bench to watch the daily procession in and out of Dr. Fuda's doors. The rural Taiwanese have no shame about watching or even blatantly staring at other people, and they practice it regularly. The bench dwellers gawk at us as we get out of the car. This part of Taiwan does not see many Anglos. Dr. Fuda is Buddhist, but he has a Daoist temple at the front of his property.

Like the others it is small with dozens of ornate statues and pots for burning incense, fake paper money, and paper talismans.

Around the side of the temple and down a dirt path past the breadfruit orchard is Dr. Fuda's clinic. It is a two-story, framed structure with aging paintwork in a color that must have passed for beige or cream some decades ago. A dozen people form a loose line in front of the simple aluminum screen door. As we approach, the screen door pops open and a little man with a short-sleeved, knot-loop shirt and slacks appears. He doesn't see us as he is busy greeting the small throng of patients. He smiles and bows his head here and there, gesturing for all of them to file in through the door. We wait patiently until the last one enters.

The old friends clap eyes on each other and smile broadly. Dr. Fuda opens his lips in a generous tea-stained, toothy grin that makes anyone within sight bubble with happiness. He walks over to our small group and appears to be genuinely grateful and happy to meet us. He is one of life's bright souls. After bowing and shaking our hands he invites us into his clinic.

Inside the door of the two-story building is a crowd of people. We stand and wait as he makes his rounds and then returns within a few minutes. He guides the group in front of us upstairs. We file along behind them. Dr. Fuda ushers us all into a large room with no furniture, then rushes off for more rounds. Slowly each person finds a place on the matted floor. First they sit, some of them talking to one another. Within a few minutes they begin to lie down on the tatami mats, heads toward the wall, feet toward the center of the room. A few people lie in the space left in the middle of the room. Next to each person is a plastic box with thin wires snaking out of it. Each of these electrostim boxes, specially built to Dr. Fuda's exact specifications, delivers a micro-current of electrical charge when attached to acupuncture needles. The chatter quiets, and a gentle, peaceful ambience ensues. Within moments of the cessation of conversation, Dr. Fuda steps into the room. His left hand clutches a bunch of acupuncture needles, fanned out at different angles like a bouquet of flowers. His eyes assess the room, taking each patient in one by one. They all begin to close their eyes and enter into a tranquil meditation as soon as he enters. All except one, a young man in his twenties who is obviously very bright. Dr. Fuda introduces him to us.

As Dr. Fuda gazes kindly at him, the young man explains that he had cancer of the nose and throat. He speaks good English. "I failed two courses of chemotherapy, and the radiation did not work. Then it metastasized to my brain. The doctors offered me another round of chemo, but I could not take it. I was getting so sick that if I started more chemotherapy or radiation I would no longer be able to hide my illness from my parents. So, I came to Dr. Fuda." I swallow hard to keep tears from welling up. I am having trouble comprehending that a young man of twenty-three years would risk his own life so he would not distress his parents. His face brightens, "That was over a year ago. Three months after Dr. Fuda's treatments started, the tumors began to shrink. Now I have had six months of clear scans. Dr. Fuda wants me to continue treatment for two years," he says. Then he closes his eyes.

Dr. Fuda slips one needle from his bouquet and, without looking, inserts it obliquely into the top of the young man's head. Within seconds he has inserted about six needles in his scalp, between his eyes, in his forearm, and between his thumb and forefinger. With deft precision he finishes needling and hooks up the wires from the plastic box to the ends of the needles. Dr. Fuda quickly flicks buttons and twists knobs on the little electric box, sending the young man's muscles into involuntary twitches and spasms. With his body gently and rhythmically convulsing, the young patient floats off into an alpha wave meditation. Dr. Fuda finishes treating eight patients within fifteen minutes and glides out of the room at speed. He has six more rooms of this size, all packed with patients. We wait in the room with the people who have just been treated.

It's as if they are all in harmony. Everyone is quiet. Their bodies are convulsing rhythmically at different rates depending upon Dr. Fuda's electrostim box settings. All their faces are peaceful.

Dr. Fuda returns twenty minutes later, motioning for us to follow. He has put the whole clinic to sleep for the moment. Dozens of patients lie on mats, beds, or tables peacefully twitching away. On the bottom floor at the far side of his clinic he has a small room with a heavy, hand-carved wooden table and chairs, set up like a bar with him on one side and everybody else on the other. He produces a huge grin and gestures for us to sit. Behind the bar Dr. Fuda prepares green tea in a tiny ceramic pot. First he places the pot in a large earthen bowl and pours boiling water over the top of it. Next he stuffs the diminutive container with leaves and then pours the hot water onto the leaves. He immediately pours the water back out of the little pot into the earthen bowl letting the passing water wash the leaves inside the pot. Again he pours hot water onto the leaves in the pot. This time he sets the pot aside while the hot water steeps the tea leaves. He places a thimble-sized ceramic cup with no handles in front of each of us. Then he picks up the pot and pours a small amount of the brew into each of our cups and finally into his own. Using both hands, he holds his tiny cup up to us. We each pick up ours with both hands and all drink at the same time.

Dr. Fuda explains that he is really a farmer. He grows prizewinning breadfruits, but because he is a Buddhist and because he took a vow to relieve pain and suffering from the world, he also does acupuncture. During the rest of the day I meet at least a dozen people who have stories like the young man's. One man shows me an ultrasound image of a mass in his liver the size of a golf ball, and then produces another image from a few months earlier of the same mass, then the size of a baseball. Breast cancer, colon cancer, stomach cancer – everyone has a story. Dr. Fuda tells me that his treatments for breast cancer and colon cancer are so successful that the patients don't need chemo or radiation therapy. He says his treatments work whether the patients have chemo or not, but the stronger drugs can make patients weak.

In the clinic, I meet a woman in her early thirties who glows with a natural beauty that would make any man or woman stop in their tracks to watch her walk by. She tells me that her husband and brother carried her into Dr. Fuda's clinic two years ago. After having multiple bowel resections, the doctors had sent her home to be with her family in her last days. Dr. Fuda says her treatment is concluded, but she still comes in twice a week anyway. He says, "Now the treatment is for her comfort."

A group of women come in. All of them have or have had breast cancer. Two patients who have been successful with Dr. Fuda's treatment argue about whether or not a third woman in their group should continue her chemotherapy. Dr. Fuda points out the interaction to me. He seems happy about it rather than upset or concerned. It's not the argument or the content, but the presence of emotional and intellectual engagement that gets his approval. His Buddhist nature allows him to be compassionate yet nonattached at the same time.

Dr. Fuda explains to me that his wife calls his clinic the "7-11" because he opens at 7 AM and doesn't finish until 11 PM. He used to take Mondays off and go to his mountain house for a rest, but now the patients have found him there as well. So he treats 40 patients before lunch on Mondays and then gets drunk in the afternoon! I like his style. I'm humbled not only by his incredible ability, but by his commitment and tremendous compassion. I spend so much time thinking about myself. He seems only to think of others. How could I ever be a healer like him?

The next day Dr. Fuda invites us to his mountain retreat, up in the hills of rural Taiwan. His retreat is in a small village, just one road with a little series of storefronts, a tiny jungle hamlet surrounded by mountains. We wind up the little road going toward his home, a few hundred feet above the village. Nestled in the side of the lush green mountainside is Dr. Fuda's retreat. It's amazingly similar to all of the other houses in southern Taiwan, a three-story job up and down, but this one has a new Mercedes-Benz parked in front, E class. The man getting out of the car notices us as we drive up; it's the husband of the woman who had bowel cancer. He looks slightly sheepish, grins, and does a half bow, then hurries into the house.

We enter through the front door. The living room has six small beds in it, forming a neat line. They all have fresh sheets with a hospital tuck. Odd decor for a living space, but its owner treats two hundred patients a day and cures cancer with acupuncture needles. Inside, the nicely dressed man with the Mercedes scurries about emptying wastebaskets and dusting; an orange apron protects his expensive clothes.

Dr. Fuda greets us with his big, beautiful smile. He opens his arms with palms facing us, then closes them again to his abdomen and bows slightly. His smile is infectious, he seems to raise everybody's spirits immediately upon entering the room. He gives us a short tour of his mountain home, beginning with the living room and then moving on to the tearoom on the same floor. His house is just like all the others in Taiwan except he has three of them joined together side by side. Then Dr. Fuda leads us up a narrow set of hardwood stairs to the second floor. It opens to a large room with a whiteboard on one wall; rows of desks and chairs fill the rest of the room. They are all made of dark, lustrous hardwood with perfect, shiny finishes.

Here is this little man with a soul the size of a mountain; he treats two hundred patients in town six days a week, and on Mondays, like today, he treats forty more in his living room. Now we're standing in front of his beautifully furnished but empty classroom. I have a sense of sadness as I stand here and look at the empty desks. Do these empty seats form part of his dream that has not yet manifested? Dr. Fuda is a Buddhist, a true Buddhist whose mission is to relieve suffering in the world. He knows he can't do it all on his own. So he wants to teach others to do the work that he does. But, as I look at these empty desks in his classroom I wonder if there are any other bodies that house souls similar to his own. Can he really teach what he does, or is the form of his practice, the acupuncture, just an empty shell that transmits the healing from his essence to his patients? Allen and Master Liao are inspired by his vision, but I am somehow left saddened by the sight.

Dr. Fuda's tour continues to the third-floor, the first place that actually looks like it could be lived in. It is a large room with comfortable, handmade, wooden furniture and a veranda that looks out over the front of the house and onto the jungle mountainside and the little village below. With his tour concluded, it's on to business. There are patients already waiting downstairs in the living room.

As we descend the stairs I hang back with Master Liao. I can't suppress my curiosity.

"Master Liao, what's the husband of the woman who was cured of bowel cancer doing here?"

"He comes to help on Mondays." says Master Liao succinctly. "Oh, when he has guests?" I ask.
"No, every Monday." He replies quietly.

"You mean he drives his Mercedes here every morning so he can empty Dr. Fuda's trash?" I ask, not realizing how vulgar and forward my open incredulity must sound to this educated Chinese man.

Taking pity on me for my ignorance, Master Liao stops on the landing and turns to me.

"This man owns a resort that caters to rich businessmen. He understands money. He knows that he cannot show his thanks to Dr. Fuda for saving his wife by only giving him money. He leaves his business every Monday morning and drives to Dr. Fuda's house early, so he can show his gratitude and humility and thanks by helping in this way." Master Liao explains.

I can only reply by closing my lips and looking at the floor. Master Liao understands in a moment the effect this revelation has had on me. I stay alone on the landing for a few minutes as the others descend. I feel small, insignificant, and arrogant. For the rest of the day Dr. Fuda is going to teach us his simple and profound acupuncture methods, but I feel that I've already had my lesson.

Commentary from Spirit

Humility is the correct response when faced with something much greater than yourself. When you realize the gift of life, of opportunity for growth, of unending love...How can this not make you humble?

My Personal Savior

Quote from Spirit

"It is with great love that we come to you. We stand patiently at the closed door of your heart."

~Rayne

I first met M, in person, on the way to a party. Malcolm pulled up in front of my house to pick me up. He had a small and varied collection of single women in his Isuzu Trooper 4x4. I don't know how he does it, must be his British charm. He never fails to be surrounded by gorgeous single women.

The passenger door opens, and there sits M, poised, elegant, and candid.

"You take the front seat, and I'll sit in back with the girls," she says.

"No, I don't mind, really," I protest, considering the possibility of spending the next forty-five minutes sitting between the two blondes in the backseat.

"Nonsense, I'll sit in the back and chat with the girls, and you sit up front and talk with Malcolm," she said in a distinctly British accent.

M was wearing a plaid, wool skirt with a conservative slit that nevertheless generously revealed her shapely, sun-tanned leg as it probed for the ground from the height of the 4x4. Using a fair portion of my willpower, I managed to meet her eyes as she exited. And remembering to act like a gentleman, I opened the back door for her, and she climbed in with the other two women. Malcolm introduced us: blonde, blonde, brunette.

"Michael, this is Marie, Sally, and Bunnie," Malcolm says. Ah, M – code name Bunnie.

"Hello, nice to meet you all," I say. "Malcolm, where we going, anyway?"

"We're going out to a ranch in the Rincon Mountains. The program is throwing a big party."

So, that's M, the mystery woman with a British accent. We all chat and enjoy the ride through the Sonoran Desert. South of Tucson, we turn onto a dusty and rutted dirt road, heading toward the Rincon Mountains. The vibration shakes the cabin of the 4x4 – too slow and the cabin jumps up and down, too fast the vibration is intolerable. Malcolm deftly finds the right speed. After a two-mile traverse through the desert we get to the gatehouse in front of the ranch. Malcolm rolls down the window.

"Dr. Riley," he speaks with authority, into the electric box. "Thank you," sounds the disembodied voice as the gate quietly swings open.

We drive another half mile on the dirt road, and then find a place to park outside the ranch. The spread consists of a medium-sized rustic contemporary house and several outbuildings, plus an organic garden and a custom-built, handcrafted tree fort. There are 50 or so people, some of them talking in small groups, some of them milling about the grounds, and a few with healthy appetites bellying up to the buffet well before serving time.

M – I mean Bunnie – and the girls wander around the ranch talking to each other. Malcolm spots a professorial looking gentleman he needs to speak to and scurries off. I stand here with the usual vague sense of panic that I feel whenever I go to a party. My first instinct is to climb up into the tree fort and stay there; instead, I force myself to be sociable. I find the host and say hello to him. He is the doctor that started the program that employs both Malcolm and myself. We share a minute or so of small talk – never my favorite thing. I'm always fascinated at how people actually enjoy parties. To me, they always seem like a forced performance.

I find Malcolm and ask who M, aka Bunnie, is talking to. "He's an ER doc who is finishing his fellowship," Malcolm says. The ER doc is tall, handsome, and tan with sandy, blond hair, tight lips, and a furrowed brow. Noticing that Bunnie is looking at us, he glances over toward Malcolm and me, looks us up and down, then turns his attention back to his conversation. Bunnie invites us over with a hand gesture.

"Malcolm and Michael, this is my friend Conner," she says. Conner says hello as he gazes just over our heads, and then turns back to Bunnie. "I'll talk to you later," he says and then exits.

Bunnie looks directly at me and asks, "Do you need a girl Friday?" I get the feeling that M knows a project when she sees one.

"What do you have in mind?" I ask.

"It's an open question," she says.

I'm not sure how to answer. Is she asking if I want to hire her? I can barely afford to pay my own bills.

"I'm afraid I'm not in a position to employ anyone right at the moment," I reply.

"Oh, I'm not looking for employment. I'm simply offering my assistance. I need something to do. I'm very organized," she says. Organized – the magic word. Is DISORGANIZED written across my forehead in capital letters? I envision the piles of paper and unanswered correspondence that litter the floor, desk, and other flat surfaces of my home office. I have a strange inability to manage paper. Some might pass it off as sheer laziness, but to me the condition is a complete enigma: I just don't have paper skills. Though I'm overjoyed at the offer, I don't let it show. Yes, expressing gratitude is a bit of a challenge for me, too.

I straighten up, look M in the eye, and say, "I would be happy to accept your offer, but it has to be Mondays, not Fridays." We shake hands.

On Monday morning the doorbell rings at 9 AM, right on the dot. M is wearing an expensive, gray wool business suit that is perfect for a high-rise law firm. I've got on a T-shirt and jeans, and no shoes. I invite her in and show her my home office setup: bathroom, waiting room, and treatment room. Then I remove the shoji screen to reveal the barren landscape of ceramic tile and the bare white walls of my open-plan living room/diningroom/kitchen. "My business office is upstairs." Bunnie follows me up. As we pass the short hallway at the landing, I hear a gasp from behind. I turn around to see her clutching at the railing on the landing. She looks pale and lightheaded.

"Are you okay," I ask.

"Oh yes, fine. There's just something there," she says. As she walks into my den of disorganization, she visibly shakes herself back to attention.

"Did you feel something there?" I ask.

"Oh, it's nothing," she replies.

"No, you felt something there didn't you?" I say.

She locks a penetrating stare onto me. "You have an unwanted visitor," Bunnie says flatly.

She feels it too. The leering frat boy that I saw – the ghost that talked to Sherri – now M feels its presence, too.

"Oh my word!" Bunnie exclaims as she surveys the various hills, mountains, and pinnacles of lost and forgotten bills, forms, and correspondence that make up the terrain of my makeshift office. She is clearly more astonished by my disorganization than by my ghost.

I make a couple of cups of tea, and then we sit on the floor and get to work. One by one we go through each stack, each file, each paper. First, everything is sorted – notes, bills, correspondence, and so on. Next, we begin the long process of dealing with each item. Nothing escapes M. Everything that I'm willing to put off, she wants to do in the moment.

After a day's work and a good portion of the paperwork done, I begin to feel a sense of relief. As Bunnie leaves she says, "I look forward to seeing you again next Monday. If you would like me to get rid of your unwanted guest, just let me know."

"What do you mean," I ask.

"Make it go away. Of course, if you would like to keep him, that is certainly up to you."

"Oh, yeah sure, that would be great. What do we need to do?"

"If it's all right, I'll come back tomorrow evening and we'll take care of it."

"Okay, how about eight?" I say.

"Eight it is."

The next evening the doorbell rings at exactly 8 PM. I open it to find Bunnie holding a small, chipped, handmade clay dish in one hand and a sprig of dried leaves in the other. She's wearing a long flowery summer dress and flat sandals. She smiles, and I invite her in.

"I hope you don't think this is too strange, but I have to do this a certain way," she says.

"No, of course, that's fine," I respond, completely bewildered but not showing it.

Bunnie walks into the living room and sits on my borrowed couch. Placing the chipped dish on her lap, she sets the sprig of dried leaves in it, rests her hands on her thighs, and closes her eyes. Her torso expands as she takes a deep breath in and exhales slowly. She is quiet for two or three minutes. When she opens her eyes they seem slightly glazed over. Without comment she retrieves a small butane lighter from the pocket of her dress. Picking up the sprig of dried leaves in her left hand, she opens the flame with her right. The dried leaves catch fire instantly, and she drops them into the earthen bowl. As the flame burns down and the dried leaves turn to embers, I notice there is some kind of powder in the bottom of the bowl. The glowing embers ignite the powder and together they give off a pungent and aromatic scent.

Without looking at me Bunnie stands up with the chipped bowl in her left hand. She begins to slowly ascend the stairs, smoke wafting behind her. I stay at the bottom and watch. When she gets to the landing she stops and begins to speak an incantation in a language that sounds like a cross between French and Spanish. At first it sounds like she is pleading with someone or something, but then her voice becomes stronger and more forceful. She continues speaking in the same language, but now it sounds like a command. Then her body shudders visibly albeit subtly. She takes a deep breath, and turns to walk back downstairs. Without looking at me, she slumps onto the couch in the exact same spot as before. After placing the chipped dish on her lap, she closes her eyes and breathes slowly and deeply for two or three minutes.

When Bunnie opens her eyes again, they seem clearer. She smiles and looks at me. "That should do it," she says.

"Is he gone?" I ask.

"He's been sent to the light," she replies.

"Oh, well, thank you," I say, not knowing what I'm supposed to do or say after an event like this.

"Yes, that should be better. I'll see you on Monday. Oh, by the way, if you're interested, I'm having a small dinner party on Thursday."

"Oh, yeah, that sounds great. What time should I be there?"

"Seven o'clock for cocktails. Dinner at seven-thirty," she says in her remarkably James Bondlike British accent.

I think, shaken not stirred, but I say, "Great! I'll see you then."

Wow! I've just been exorcised – well, not me, but the ghost in my house. After Bunnie has gone, I sit on the couch, looking up at the empty stair landing. Did she really send the ghost into the light? Was there really a ghost? That makes three of us now who have noticed it – Sherri, Bunnie, and myself. I didn't tell either of them about it before they noticed it on their own. It can't all be in our imagination. Can it? Bunnie, with her James Bond accent and gray wool business suit, is the last person in the world I would imagine to be an exorcist.

When I show up to Bunnie's house for dinner on Thursday I notice a red BMW M3 E30 Lightweight parked in the driveway: the last of the light and nimble saloon cars. I prefer two-seaters, but there is a place in my heart for M-class Bimmers. I pull up to the curb and turn off my motor to wait for a minute before going in. I take a breath and gather up my social skills. Just as I'm getting out of my car, the doctor from the party strides out of Bunnie's house. Lips tight, brow furrowed – the same way he looked at the party. I walk toward the house, and he passes me on the way in. This time Dr. Handsome forgoes salutations completely, instead offering me a brief, but cold, stare and an audible, but incomprehensible, utterance that passes for a grunt as he heads to his Bimmer.

Bunnie meets me at the door. She's wearing a red leather skirt, white blouse, nylons, and red heels. I know there was something going on with her and Dr. Handsome a moment ago, but she maintains perfect composure. She smiles and invites me in. Bunnie shows me into the living room where a few guests are drinking and talking, and then she hurries back into the kitchen. Malcolm is here with a date – another blonde, a new one this time. There are a couple of fellowship doctors from the program, one small and one big; quiet and loud, man and woman, respectively. The quiet one, thin with sallow skin, writes books about health.

A few minutes later, Bunnie announces, "Dinner is served."

We file in from the living room and sit around the glass dining table – boy, girl, boy, girl. I sit between Bunnie and Malcolm's date, with the sallow-skinned health author directly across from me and the loud woman to the diagonal. The table is impeccably set with more forks and spoons than I'm used to. The meal is excellent – broiled salmon, new potatoes, fresh vegetables, salad, and coconut sorbet served in real coconut shells. I find myself switching between being a spectator and being a normal, sociable person.

As a spectator I see Malcolm trying to charm his date, the sallow-skinned health author drooling over Bunnie, and the loud woman trying to assess which of the three men she could take home with her tonight. I even see myself sitting here, trying to look calm and interested at the same time; but inside I feel wound up, tense, and anxious. All the while, Bunnie delicately and deftly shuffles the food and the conversation, the perfect hostess.

Dinner wraps up early, and, as everyone has a place to go except me, I find myself the last guest to leave.

"Can I help clean up?" I ask.

"No, I'll just turn off the lights and pretend it's already cleaned up," Bunnie responds with a smile.

We sit on a leather couch in the living room. I'm curious about the ghost she cleared from my house and what she did with it. The whole house did feel different after she did her exorcism thing.

"Thank you for your help the other day. My house definitely seems lighter," I say.

"It was nothing," she says.

"It was definitely something. Where did you learn it?" I ask a bit too sharply.

"You seem a little tense. Do you feel all right?" she asks. She's trying to change the subject, but she's right, I can feel the tension all over my body. I think I've been like this all my life, but I spend so much of my time trying to look cool that I close my own mind to how I actually feel. Most people don't notice that about me. She definitely has some insight. "No, I'm fine, thanks," I say.

"I can help with that too, you know," she says.

"Help with what?" I ask, trying not to look like a deer in headlights.

"The tension in your body. Do you know where it comes from?" she asks.

"No, really, I'm fine," I say.

"Hmm, I see," she says. "I noticed your patients like you very much, but you don't have many of them," changing the subject again.

Ouch! Okay, I can take the good with the bad. I always try to do my best for the people I work with, but she's got me – I'm barely making a living. I guess I have to face the fact that I'm a terrible businessman, evidenced by the hills and mountains of forgotten paperwork cached in my home office – that and my bank statements.

"Um, well, yeah, I'd really like to build my practice," I say.
"I'd like to show you something. Do you trust me?"
Do I trust her? Why would I have to trust her? But I do, actually.
"Sure, I trust you."

"I lived in Brazil for 15 years. People are very close to spirit there. I worked in a spiritual teaching center. If you let me, I can help to take away some of the tension you carry with you."

Okay, I'm game. Is she going to exorcise me, too? No, that's stupid – or is it?

"It will only take a few minutes. If you'd like to just lie down on the sofa, I'll be right back," she says.

I lie down onto the leather couch and fold my hands over my abdomen and wonder what's coming next. Bunnie glides back into the room holding a glass of water in her left hand. In her right hand is a red string with a clear quartz crystal tied to the end. The string is wrapped haphazardly around the crystal and has several knots in it to secure its position. She has the same slightly glazed-over look in her eyes again, as she did when she sent the spirit away from my stair landing. She looks down at me, or rather through me, or, maybe, into me.

"Hands at your sides, please. Close your eyes," she says.

I close my eyes, mostly. Through my eyelashes, I can see that she is still holding the cup of water in her left hand. She's holding the cup by the rim, with two fingers dipping into the water and the thumb on the outside so the glass is pinched between her fingers. With her right hand she dangles the crystal over my pelvis. The crystal begins to swing in a wide circle. In a few minutes she moves the crystal up a few inches toward my bellybutton. It begins to swing again. Over my heart, the pendulum jumps and swings wildly. It looks like she's making a stop at each of the seven major chakras. The crystal swings and rotates over each of the areas. By the time she gets to the top of my head, all the tension has left my body.

"They have cleared your chakras. Now, they will put energy in," she says in a faraway voice.

They? Okay, I'm just going to go with the flow. Something is definitely happening. I'm feeling really comfortable, relaxed, even peaceful. She repeats the same process from bottom to top. This time she lingers at the top chakra, the Crown. She starts speaking quietly in the same foreign language, a cross between French and Spanish. Then she convulses ever so slightly and takes in an audible breath. She walks out of the room without saying anything.

I feel incredibly comfortable. I don't know if I want to go to sleep or go for a run. I am relaxed but at the same time energized. I sit up and look out through the same eyes, but I feel like I see things differently. Everything just feels natural, like it should. This is what I'm supposed to feel like, my natural self. What did she do?

She comes back into the room looking normal again, eyes clear and animated.

"Thank you," I say, noticing a new resonance in my chest as I speak.

"Not at all," M is back. Very British.

"What language were you speaking?"

"In Brazil we speak Portuguese."

"Really, it's a very beautiful language. Well, thank you so much. I feel much better. Thank you for dinner, also. It was excellent."

"Oh, it was just a little something," she says, still very British. "Do I get to see you again on Monday?" I ask.
"Of course, 9 AM," she says, matter-of-factly.
"Great, I'll see you then."

Outside, I hop into my topdown convertible without opening the door. Very cheesy, like some suave guy in a movie, but it's fun. The asphalt on First Avenue is fresh and smooth. The road rises and falls, gently undulating underneath as I cruise south from the foothills toward River Road. The night is glorious, stars twinkle above and the lights of Tucson twinkle below. At River Road the left-turn light is green and the intersection is empty. With a blip of the throttle I downshift to third and accelerate through the corner. I feel G-forces gently pull the fluids to the right side of my body as I power through the turn. As the road straightens, I ease off the throttle, trying to stay within the speed limit. I feel good. I feel like me.

Commentary from Spirit

Throughout your lifetime, individuals will be sent to you. They are here to help with your spiritual progress. They may be your friend, your adversary, your lover, or your brother. However they manifest, learn to recognize those who have been sent for you.

The Big House

Quote from Spirit
The gift will be given. You must see it and you must act.
~William

Bunnie continues to organize my life on Mondays. A little more money is coming in, and patient bookings seem to be more consistent. I'm still amazed and intrigued by Bunnie's blend of gifts, skills, and mannerisms. Monday is becoming my favorite day. After a few short weeks she has transformed the maze of forgotten paperwork and indiscriminate stacks of correspondence that was my office into an organized and efficient space for getting things done. With my life organized and a few more pendulum and chakra treatments under my belt, I feel ready to take on something new.

Another interesting thing about Bunnie is that she drives as fast as I do. I have to admit, though, I do feel safer when I'm the one behind the wheel. It's another clear and sunny day in the Sonoran Desert. We've just left Ventana Canyon heading south, then take a right on River Road. A quick joyride with the top down, enjoying the Sunday morning, and wondering where we should go for lunch. We've always got something to talk about.

"I feel like I've got to work again," she says. "You mean your spiritual work?" I ask.
"It's time, I can feel it," she says.

"Then wouldn't it be cool if we had a big house with a beautiful garden and a relaxed vibe, kind of like a spa, but more like a home, to do our work?" I say.

"There's a house!" She yells, just as we are starting down my favorite corkscrew turn on River Road just past Swan.

"Let's check it out!" I say.

"Oh, no. I'm sure it's nothing. That's stupid. We're just talking," she says.

"Let's check it out anyway," I say.

At the bottom of the corkscrew I find a wide spot to whip around and drive back up the hill. I turn left across River Road toward the mountains into the driveway. We pass the small, broken-down real estate sign, which has fallen to the ground, and continue down the driveway, which crosses a dry desert wash and then climbs back up again to meet a large pair of iron swinging gates. The gates, painted green with the initials G.G. on them, are closed.

The main driveway – landscaped with native Sonoran vegetation, nopalitos, saguaros, mesquites and blue palo verdes – continues up past the gates. We can see the south end of the house – pale yellow stucco with a Spanish tile roof and a veranda that looks like it came from a chateau in the south of France. On the gate is attached a small sign with the real estate agent's phone number. It's barely legible, and the sign looks like it's been there forever. I punch in the numbers on my cell phone and ready myself with my best businesslike voice.

"Hello, this is Wanda," speaks the tight, shrill voice on the other end.

"Hi. I'm outside your house on River and Swan."

"You don't want it. It's too big, the HVAC is antiquated, and kitchen needs updating," she says sharply.

Wow! That's an interesting sales pitch. She must really hate the place.

"Can we view it tomorrow morning at 8 AM?" I am surprised to hear the words coming out of my mouth. There's no way we could afford this giant monster of a house.

"Okay, I'll meet you there at eight, but put an hour aside, so after we see the house I can take you to some other place that you might actually buy," she says, in a tired and fed-up tone.

"Okay, we'll be there," I reply and hang up. "That was interesting."

In the evening, out of the blue, Bunnie checks her answering machine to find a message from a different real estate agent representing a client who wants to buy her house even though it is not on the market. The client likes the neighborhood and just lost a contract on a nearby house. He makes a generous site-unseen offer. The only catch is Bunnie has to agree to a fifteen-day closing time. I can feel the acceleration.

The next morning we meet the real estate agent at 8 AM. We drive up the gently bending, gravel drive as it meanders through the grounds up to the front of the house. There are huge metal sculptures planted around the two-acre front yard. There must be at least twelve or fifteen of them distributed among the brush and cacti, the smaller ones are inspired renderings of the natural vegetation. Others, twelve or fifteen feet tall, are made of iron bars and tubes shaped into lightning bolts and bells, bent and twisted into artistic statements.

The house is huge with a separate five-car garage. I don't think I have ever seen a five-car garage before. The big, sprawling eight-thousand-square-foot home was built by an eccentric who was an interior designer and art collector. Huge, colorful, and sometimes garish oil paintings still cover some of the interior walls. There is room for multiple living quarters plus an entire wing with five rooms that can be devoted to the clinic.

We learn that the house has been on the market for over two years. The owner died and the heirs could not agree on a final price.

Shortly before we drove by, the sale of the house was turned over to the family lawyers. Being the last item in probate made it a hot potato they couldn't wait to get rid of. We make an offer at fifty percent of the asking price. Seven counteroffers later, it is accepted. I sell everything I own and get the biggest mortgage I've ever had just to cover my half. Now, I really have to work!

Once we get the practice moved into the new house, my bookings start to increase. Patients seem to want to hang around and just enjoy the atmosphere, even after their treatments are finished. Some even say that they start to feel better the moment they drive through the gates. Sometimes, when it's quiet in the house, I feel energy pulsate like an electrical generator. I have to wonder if this house was just waiting for us to drive by so it could call out to us.

Commentary from Spirit

At times in your life you will be offered a favorable moment that makes your next step possible. It often involves recognition followed by hard work.

Keep your eyes open for the opportunities that are periodically handed to you. Act swiftly and decisively to seize the moment.

Jungle Man

Quote from Spirit
"Come all you seekers and find."
~William

I feel like an imposter, living in an 8,000 square-foot house on four acres in the Tucson foothills. Six months after moving to River Road, my acupuncture practice has tripled in size and doctors from the university are asking to observe my work with patients. I have all the trappings of success, even the right zip code, yet, inside, I feel the same fears and insecurities that I have always felt. Am I always going to be this way? Rich or poor, successful or unsuccessful, does my inner being change as my outer environment changes or does it stay the same?

My morning commute to work is a walk of about sixty steps from my bedroom to the foyer, which functions as the reception area to the clinic. Bunnie manages the office when she isn't quietly practicing her own form of spiritual therapy. She is already in the office when I arrive, and she points to a DVD on the front desk left by our friend Cynthia.

"I think it's very important that we watch this."

"Why?" I ask.

"I've known Cynthia for a long time and she always gives me things just at the time I need them."

"Okay, let's watch it tonight."

After clinic we watch a video of an incredible Brazilian healer who does amazing things like cutting people open and removing their tumors as they stand in line chatting with him. The person being cut appears to feel no pain and hardly bleeds at all. The healer, known as John of God, claims that the true healing is spiritual. He does physical surgery only for those who don't believe that direct spiritual intervention is possible. He surmises that if they see him performing feats that seem miraculous then they will find it easier to embrace spirituality, but he reiterates that true healing comes only from God.

The next week we read a book about John of God. We find out that this amazing healer has a distant association with the same Spiritist group that Bunnie trained with in Brazil. We are so impressed with what we saw in the video that we decide to travel and see him with our own eyes.

Two weeks later we land in Brasilia, the capital of Brazil. A driver was supposed to meet us here, but he hasn't shown up. Our cell phones have no service here, so we find a payphone, but we can't make it work either. Bunnie lived in Sao Paulo for fifteen years. I'm grateful that she speaks Portuguese fluently. Relying on the kindness of strangers, she asks a well-dressed Brazilian man to help us with the phone. He responds in a gracious manner, but he also is unable to make the payphone work. Embarrassed, he confers with his friend briefly, then reaches inside his suit pocket and produces an identification badge.

"I am Senhor Macedo, the chief of police of Brasilia. I'm sorry you had trouble with the phone. Is there any other way I could help you?" He asks very politely.

I'm amazed. While Bunnie tells him we're trying to get to a little town called Abadiania, I'm trying to imagine how differently things might have gone had we accosted the Chief of Police of Washington, D.C., to ask him to use his cell phone and ask directions to Boonsboro. He walks with us out to the curb where taxicabs are lined up. Leaning into the window of the next open taxi, he shows his ID to the driver, and then instructs him to take us to Abadiania and charge us a flat rate. I'm relieved that he thought of this detail.

Most taxi drivers in Brazil are honest, but I dread the thought of being fifty miles out of town and then having to renegotiate the rate.

An hour and a half later we arrive in the small rural town of Abadiania. It's a one-road town that has built up around the clinic of the healer, John of God. His compound is called the Casa de Dom Ignacio. It is claimed that he sees between 500 and 1,000 people per day.

The taxi drops us off in the middle of the night at a little bed and breakfast, called a pousada. Two kind, round faces appear at the door. They ask if we want to share a room with others or if we would prefer a room each. We opt for private rooms.

My room is very small, filled mostly by a cot with wooden slats and a thin mattress. Behind a flimsy metal door in the corner of the room is a bathroom. It's a small cubicle with a toilet and a makeshift plastic basin hanging loosely on the wall. A plastic pipe from the ceiling comes down the wall and ends with a small on-off lever just above the basin. In the corner there is a drain in the floor, and several feet directly above it hangs a plastic shower head about the size of a coffee pot. From the top of the shower head protrude two electrical wires whose ends are twisted together and attached to the main power line with precariously-wrapped electrical tape. Certain ceath.

In the morning I venture out of my cell. In the front room of the pousada I find a table covered with an old-fashioned, red checker tablecloth and laid with fresh tropical fruits – mango, papaya, and pineapple. But no banana; John of God has forbidden the eating of bananas. There is also cheese, fresh bread, and cakes. The breakfast room is full of people of many nationalities – American, Indian, German, French, even Russian. They are from completely different cultures, yet they are all united by their quest for spiritual and physical healing from John of God.

After breakfast Bunnie and I walk down the road toward the Casa. People of all sizes, shapes, and colors – all dressed in white, the preferred color of John of God – fill the road in this tiny rural town. They walk at an unusually slow pace. Some are bent. Some are upright. A few push others in wheelchairs. A river of white cloth flows toward the Casa de Dom Ignacio. Pousadas dot the road on the way. Between them are small storefronts offering locally-made clothing, artwork, and trinkets for sale. Street vendors hawk freshly- roasted cashews to the migrating masses. In an open field along the side of the road a large stage is being built. Above it a huge banner reads, "Happy Birthday!" We have arrived on the birthday of the healer, John of God.

A bit further up the road throngs of people clad in white are filing into the Casa. The grounds with the lawns, flowers, and shrubs are beautifully kept. At the edge of the compound is a meditation deck that offers a peaceful view of a valley as it spills out below the Casa.

Brazilians from all over the country pour out of large buses parked in front of the Casa. Most of them are poor – not American poor, but truly poor. Threadbare clothing with multiple patchwork repairs and the lack of luggage suggest they own little more than what they are wearing. I see the wizened face of a man more than twice my age. He looks at me with ancient eyes creased by hardship, toil, and love. In a brief and silent glance he transmits a quiet revelation into my mind.

I am poor. You are rich. I am old. You are young. I have no opportunities. You have all the doors open to you, yet the door to your heart is closed. Because of that, in my humility, I open my heart to yours.

The old man walks on to enter the Casa, but I stop in my tracks. Normally, I would question my perception of another's thoughts, but the old man's thoughts literally jumped into my head. They were not my thoughts – they were his. With a mere glance I am stricken by the many disparities between us. I have to tear my self away from this spot or I will be here in contemplation for the rest of the day.

Inside the main hall Bunnie and I line up with hundreds of other souls. They range from perfectly healthy to desperately ill, from spiritual voyeurs to pious believers. After two hours in the slow-moving line, I find a small seat next to the stage where people are giving enthusiastic and animated speeches about spirituality in both English and Portuguese. I sit to rest my aching feet. Behind me, a few people back in line, stands a woman in her 80s. I immediately stand up to offer her my seat, but she doesn't understand me. A younger woman translates for her.

"She doesn't understand English," the young woman says.

"Oh, I just wanted to offer her my seat," I say.

The young woman relays my message to the old woman, but this is Brazil, so within seconds there are four women assisting in the discussion. The old woman pushes through them toward me, with her hands clasped in front of her clutching a wooden rosary. She opens her hands to encompass my own hands. She looks me directly in the eyes as I feel the point of the wooden cross gently digging into the back of my wrist. She speaks to me and the young woman translates.

"You are a kind young man, but I am sorry that I cannot accept your offer, because my knees are crippled with arthritis and I have too much pain to sit down."

I hold the old woman's hands for a moment, smile at her and her helpers, and then take my seat. After listening to the speeches for a few more minutes, I stand up and rejoin the line as it continues to inch forward. The speaker on the stage admonishes us to be kind to all and to seek only humility for our selves. I should probably go home. I've already had all the humility I can handle for one trip.

Finally, the line advances and Bunnie and I are standing in front of the door to the room where the healer sits. When the door opens, we step through into a room where a hundred people dressed in white are sitting in meditation like a field of white poppies. The peaceful music of Ave Maria is playing through speakers. The mood is solemn, yet energized. The line continues on in front of me and snakes around the corner through the field of meditators. As we move along around the corner, I can see John of God sitting in his chair, briefly talking to each person who passes him. When I get in front of him, he looks into me with wide-set, pale blue eyes—not at me, but into me.

"Go home and help people. We will be with you," he says through a translator as he hands me a small slip of paper.

I'm quickly ushered out of the room by an assistant and told that I need to come back for an operation. An operation? Instantly I feel fear, remembering the video that showed him scraping someone's eyeball with a scalpel while they stood there smiling. The attendant can see the trepidation on my face and assures me that this will be a spiritual operation, not a physical operation. I am relieved.

Outside, I find Bunnie and learn that she, too, is scheduled for a spiritual operation. We are directed to an area where soup is served. Everyone who visits the Casa is offered a bowl of vegetable soup and a crust of bread. There is no charge for this, nor is there any charge to see John of God.

As I look around at the outdoor tables where people are seated to take their soup, I see the old man from the bus sitting quietly by himself, dipping the crust of bread into his bowl. This is probably the only meal he will have today. At the table nearest the soup kiosk sits an obese American woman. Her voice is loud and shrill.

"Well, if this is all they're going to give us, it's just not going to be enough," she cackles in a loud, squeaky voice.

We eat quietly and make our way back to the pousada. In my room I find literature stating that San Ignacio de Loyola, the founder of the Jesuits, comes through the body of the medium John of God to do healing work. The spirits of physicians, named Dr. Augusto and Dr. Oswaldo Cruz, and others also do healing work through his body. I'm not sure what to think of this. Anything is possible, I suppose, but some things seem highly improbable. Between the jet lag and the long day of standing in line I'm tired, so I go to sleep shortly after dinner.

In the morning we line up again in the main hall at the Casa. A couple of hours later we find ourselves filing by John of God again. He doesn't speak to us this time, but waves us by. I look at him and, to my astonishment, his eyes are not blue today but brown. Is this a sign that a different spirit has come through his body today? After we pass him we are invited to sit in the operation room. There are twelve of us in the room. We are instructed to be silent and sit with our eyes closed. Within seconds wild colors begin to dance on the dark screen of my eyelids, and then I feel a pinch deep inside my gut just to the left of my navel, and then another deep pinch to the right. After only a couple of minutes we are asked to stand up and leave the room. But when I stand, I feel like I shouldn't straighten up completely. A sense deep inside my gut tells me to be gentle with myself or I run the risk of suffering internal damage.

I slowly walk out of the operation room and find Bunnie already outside on the sidewalk doubled over as if she'd just been socked in the stomach. When I put my arm around her and ask if she's okay, she looks at me through glassy eyes as if she can barely see me.

"I need to lie down," she says.
"Here?" I ask.
"No, back at the Pousada," she replies in a faraway voice.

Like walking wounded, we prop each other up and precariously hobble several hundred yards back to the pousada. I crawl into my lumpy little cot, and pull the thin sheet over me. I drift into a deep, hypnotic, sleep-like trance. Time ceases to have meaning. I don't leave the room for 24 hours. I feel like if I move too fast or do something too strenuous I will damage my insides. Maybe it's my imagination, but that's how I feel. I also feel extremely fatigued.

Only the next afternoon do we both feel safe to emerge from our confines. Bunnie is able to stand up straight again and walk without assistance. She tells me she felt the same sort of pinch that I felt during the operation, but hers was lower in the pelvic area.

Against the advice of the Casa to rest for three days after spiritual surgery, we catch a flight the next day to the city of Manaus in the state of Amazonas. We're not averse to the advice, but we had already booked our stay at the eco-resort in the Amazon.

*

Manaus is at the edge of the jungle along the Rio Negro where it meets the Amazon. The air is heavy, hot, and sticky. This modern-day city started out as a fort settled by Europeans in 1669. Now, it is the most populous city in Amazonas with 1.5 million people, a bustling economy, and a free port where goods are traded without taxation. It is the largest city in northern Brazil.

After we land, a car meets us at the airport and we are taken to a grand colonial-style hotel. It used to be part of the world tour for young aristocrats years ago. We stay one night in the 19th century hotel. Everything in our rooms save for the mattress and bedding is handmade from deep, dark, and lustrous Brazilian hardwoods. Although the hotel is beautiful, it is not comfortable. In the morning we are happy to leave.

We are taken by car to a boat launch on the bank of the Rio Negro. We spend an hour going downriver in an aging wooden boat with its outboard motor spewing black smoke into the moist air, and then our boat veers right to continue up the Amazon. The water turns from the very dark, almost black, water of the Rio Negro to a greenish brown. The air is heavy and thick, hot and stifling. The banks on both sides of the river are thick with dense, green jungle. After another hour continuing upstream we see a clearing hacked out of the rainforest. It has a small shoreline, an open-air building with a thatched roof, and several small huts dotted around it.

On the shore we are met by a middle-aged Brazilian woman who speaks little English. She directs two young boys to take our bags to our cabins. We follow them up the winding path to our quaint, little, one-room bungalows. Inside each are a bed and a sink. The bathroom is outside. The walls are thin, made of woven leaves, and the windows have screens but no glass. I splash some water on my face and then head back down to the open-air building where they are setting up for lunch.

We seem to be the only guests, yet the buffet is set for at least a dozen. Our hostess explains that today we have a rare treat, vegetarian fish. No, it's not an oxymoron, the fish itself is a vegetarian. This particular fish eats only fruit that has fallen from trees into the water. Before we can sit down we are introduced to our jungle guide. He is one of the indigenous people. He is short, dark brown, quiet, and sullen. He speaks little English but the hostess insists that he dine with us at our table, just the three of us.

We fill our plates with food and return to the table. Our guide opens a large bottle of fresh water and pours it into our glasses, but he leaves his own glass empty. He explains that he does not take any liquids thirty minutes before or thirty minutes after eating. During our meal more guests show up for the buffet – a young European couple and a German family; husband, wife, and two children, boy and girl. To each set of guests a different guide is assigned. Ours has distinctly different features than the other two, who are taller, lighter-skinned, cheerful, and engaging. We enjoy our meal with very little conversation. The vegetarian fish is meaty and sweet.

After lunch we all walk down to the shore where two small motorboats and one handmade canoe are moored along the sandy shore of the great river. As the other guests get into the motorboats, our guide directs us to his canoe. He is wearing a large machete on his belt.

"You have laptop?" he asks.

"Yes," I answer.

"This is my laptop," he barks, patting the scabbard on his belt.

"Hey," he yells to his fellow guides. "You know why I can do things that you can't do?" He taunts. The other two guides look at him and say nothing.

"Because I am a jungle man!" he announces, poking his fingertips to his sternum.

We climb into the center of the canoe and sit in single line, front to back on the thin wooden blank seats. Our guide pushes off and then leaps like a cat into the front. Sitting cross-legged at the bow of his little craft, he produces a small hand-carved paddle and quietly dips it into the water as the buzz of the other two motors wanes off in the distance.

We slip quietly across the Amazon to the shore on the other side where the motorboats have already docked. Hopping out of his canoe, our guide pulls it ashore and directs us with his machete towards an open-air jungle gym made of bamboo where monkeys are congregating. He hands us a small bag of nuts and sits on the decaying stump of a felled hardwood tree. We follow the other guests to the monkeys.

The German man is trying to coax a monkey onto his shoulder and at the same time telling his wife to make sure she gets it in the video. The young couple toss nuts to the monkeys one-by-one, making them catch them in midair. We set our bag of nuts on a post and walk away, finding our own log to sit on.

Our guide does not mingle with the other two guides. He keeps his distance, quietly watching everyone. After a few minutes he approaches us and straddles our log at the far end facing us. With no preamble and in broken English he begins speaking to us.

"You should wear red," he states.

We both look at each other, but say nothing.

"You have power and you are both healers. People will be jealous of you, so you should wear red for protection."

He stands up, turns around, and walks back to his canoe. We leave the others with the monkeys and follow him. Silently, we cross the river to the other shore.

"When the Sun goes down, meet me here," he says, smacking the wide blade of his machete onto his palm. Then he turns and walks away.

The night is dark and the jungle is loud. It hisses, buzzes, clicks, and snaps. With mosquitoes whirring around our ears, we tread carefully toward the shore. It's so dark, we can barely see to get into the canoe.

Our guide silently and effortlessly dips his paddle into the dark water, compelling the canoe into the blackness as the night surrounds us. Within seconds, we are completely disoriented and don't know where we are on the river. We feel a decisive shift in direction as the canoe glides on a new trajectory. Soon the canoe slows, and suddenly I hear the machete hacking through vines and branches. As my eyes begin to adjust to the blackness, I can see branches and thick vines all around us. The canoe is now weaving very slowly through mangrove swamps. Then, we stop.

A chill of terror seizes me. I'm forced to consider the fact that we are in the middle of nowhere, lost in the dark, unarmed, and at the mercy of a jungle man with a razor-sharp laptop. All at once there is a splash of water and a flurry of motion. Bunnie and I sit frozen, our white knuckles gripping the edge of the canoe. In the next instant all goes quiet. We don't speak. We don't move.

We see the silhouette of the jungle man sitting at the front of the canoe, but now he's facing us. He has something in his lap and is stroking it horizontally.

"Come see," he says.

We move closer. In the darkness we can just make out what is on his lap. He is cradling a small crocodile about three and a half feet long on his knees. His machete is still in his belt and there's no blood on the dangerous creature. He gently strokes its belly, then invites us to do the same. Its skin is cool and smooth to the touch. After a few minutes our guide shoos us away with the back of his hand. We sit back in our places in the canoe as he lifts the crocodile from his lap and places it back into the black water. There is a splash and flurry of movement. The crocodile returns to its habitat as the jungle man sits quietly at the head of the canoe. With seemingly no effort, he extracts us from the dense jungle and deposits us back onto the shore where we began. We are left to our own devices to find our way in the dark back to our bungalows.

I've had diarrhea for two days now and it is getting worse. Pure water is flushing through my guts. I'm dehydrated and weak, and I'm sure I'm losing weight. In the morning we tell the jungle man of my predicament. He looks at me thoughtfully for a moment then disappears into the jungle. Fifteen minutes later he reappears holding a handful of green leaves in his right hand. He crushes the leaves, drops them into an empty thermos, and then pours boiling water from a tin kettle into it. He screws the top on the thermos and sets it on our table. Finally, he pours some of the boiling water into a glass and crushes a few more of the green leaves into the water.

"Drink this now," he says, pointing to the glass of tannish colored, herbal infused water.

"Take this all day," he says, pointing to the thermos.

"Thank you," I say, as he walks away.

The tea is bitter-tasting and smells musty, but I drink it anyway. I feel better instantly. Either it's a miraculous cure or it's my imagination. I carry the infusion with me and sip it for the rest of the day. By evening I haven't had to visit the toilet a single time. My diarrhea is completely cured.

The next morning it's time for us to leave, and our guide is nowhere to be found. Loading our suitcases into the motorboats, we jump in and settle down for the return journey down the Amazon and across the black water of the Rio Negro to Manaus. As the boat sputters down the river, the driver points to the silhouette of a toucan sitting at the top of the jungle canopy. It takes a few minutes to focus on the tiny outline of the bird above the trees. His profile shows his massive beak in silhouette against silver grey clouds. As my eyes follow the jungle canopy down to the bank of the Rio Negro, I see a lone figure with both arms at his sides. He is standing in front of his canoe watching as our little boat carries us out of his world.

*

Back at the Casa de Dom Ignacio, I am spending more time alone. I have given up on trying to know if I'm imagining things. The experiences I have been having are so vivid, so real, and so intense that it is out of the question to deny them. Today is Tuesday, so the Casa is quiet. It is only open officially on Wednesday, Thursday, and Friday. I take advantage of the calm atmosphere to reflect on my experiences of the last few days. I wander to the edge of the compound and sit on a bench on the meditation deck. In front of me the valley gently falls away. A light, gentle, and warm breeze caresses my face. As I look out over the valley my mind begins to relax. As soon as my mind stops working I begin to feel a peculiar sensation. Emotions are raining down onto me from far above. Compassion, love, and joy are falling down onto me like glittering raindrops. It's overwhelming. I can feel the rhythm of my breath speeding up as my body trembles gently. A light sweat breaks out over my skin. My lower lip trembles. Small jolts of electricity spark through my body and I feel my muscles twitch with each of them. I can hear a quiet, high-pitched whimper emanating from my own mouth. I feel like my heart is going to break open. I'm unequipped to handle this level of emotional intensity. I'm having a spiritual revelation right here on this wooden bench out in the open. There is no church, no priest, and no healer. I'm on my own and I feel extraordinarily vulnerable. And then, suddenly, I am released. The intense emotional rain ceases. The weather in Abadiania has not changed, but a storm of emotion has passed through me leaving me both exhausted and renewed at the same time.

What does all this mean? Am I being initiated in some way? Am I supposed to stay here in Abadiania and continue my spiritual journey? As these thoughts go through my head, I feel an energy coming down from above me again, an energy distinctly different from the one a few moments ago. I feel two hands on my shoulders gently pushing me up and forward, almost pushing me off my seat, but there is nobody behind me. A voice in my head says, "Go home and help people. We will be with you." Suddenly, my mind is perfectly clear. My questions have been answered with these words. My future, my destiny, is to continue to use my skills to help people. Does everyone have a destiny? Is there some specific task or function that each person should be doing in their lifetime – a kind of spiritual purpose?

Commentary from Spirit

Do not imagine that real spiritual interactions only exist in books or in the pages of religious history. You are capable of having spiritual experiences now. Spirits are working tirelessly to help you all the time everywhere. They are also "nearer the surface," in certain areas and around certain people who can act as channels for their energy.
Seek in your own way and discover there is an abundance of spiritual energy, information, and help at your disposal.

The Witch is Dead

Quote from Spirit

"You have friends from afar. We reach out to you when you are in need. Accept our help."
~William

Traveling thirty-six hours straight, door-to-door from the Casa de Dom Ignacio in rural Brazil to our house on River Road in Tucson would have left us completely exhausted under normal circumstances, but there is little that can be considered normal about our experiences of the past two weeks. We arrive home in Tucson feeling happy and invigorated.

We are met at the door by Walt, a mature gentleman who has been my Chinese medicine apprentice for the past year. His father is a doctor and his grandfather was a homoeopath. Starting on his second career, in Chinese medicine, Walt will eventually become an acupuncturist. He stays at the house and manages the office when we travel. It's midmorning, and, still bleary-eyed after a night's sleep, Walt looks at us with some amazement. I can see the gears cranking up to speed in his brain. "Wait a minute, why am I tired and they are refreshed? I just had a night's sleep and they just got off of an all- night flight. Hmm, there is something different about them..." So goes the monologue in his head.

"Hello, Walt!" Bunnie says.

"Hi, you guys. Whoa, are you sure you just got off an all-night flight? You look great."

"We feel great. Let's dump our stuff and get brunch at The Grill," I say.

"Are you sure? I thought you'd want some time to recuperate."

Though we've just completed thirty-six hours of taxis, airplane flights, and shuttle busses, Bunnie and I feel fresh, clear, and full of energy. So instead of heading straight to bed for a twelve-hour nap, I quickly phone Charles and Peggy, and Oswald and Sherri, to join the three of us for brunch in the Tucson foothills at The Grill at Hacienda del Sol, which has a beautiful panoramic view of the Santa Catalina mountain range and a fantastic buffet.

Our friends can't believe we've been traveling for thirty-six hours and still feel like meeting them for lunch. We are radiating like we've been plugged into a light socket as we tell the story of our adventure to our friends. Charles shifts uneasily in his chair and smiles, while Peggy beams an incredulous grin at me; they both quietly decide never to go to the Casa de Dom Ignacio. Oswald is fascinated, and Sherri thinks our story is perfectly plausible, but then she buys lucky charms from Balinese priests and talks to ghosts. They will probably be at the Casa within the year. Walt quietly takes in our story. Whatever our friends' opinions, they all seem to agree that something has changed within us, although no one can really put their finger on it.

As the weeks go by, I begin to feel more like my old self. It's hard to tell whether I'm getting used to the changes that happened to me or I'm just reverting back to how I was. Some of the radiant glow has definitely left me, but I feel like my eyes continue to see more than they had before, especially with patients. I don't see green troll heads poking out from people's necks or spinning chakras whizzing out from their bodies. It's subtler. I feel like I'm understanding my patients better. I find myself not only sensing their energy with my hands, but I'm also seeing images from their pasts and feeling emotions that they have tucked safely away over time.

One of my patients is an elderly woman who has trouble sitting, walking, and sleeping because of hip pain. I'm able to select some acupuncture points on her hand that relieve the pain. But, when I touch the points, I also see an image in my own head of women, sitting around in a semicircle, who look like they are sewing or knitting. It's not only an image; it's a feeling, too. It's a complete emotional experience. I can feel a sense of joy, love, and safety. It must be a feeling that she felt when she was in the bosom of her family. Still not willing to take these images and feelings as fact without getting some kind of verification, I ask her about the sewing circle and the good feelings she had at that time in her life. She is surprised, and she asks how I would know about that. I tell her that I can see it through the acupuncture needle. Thankfully, she is not freaked out about this revelation. She asks how I can see that through the acupuncture needle. I don't know how to answer her. She asks what it has to do with her hip pain, and I don't know how to answer that either, but I continue getting more and more of these types of insights as I work with my patients.

One day a man in his fifties who works in the music industry comes into the clinic. The music man has various complaints – back pain, digestive issues, etc., – none of which are serious, but I can sense something uncomfortable in his energy. After responding to my usual list of questions, he gets onto the treatment table and I begin to let my hands assess his energy. I touch his energy from the outer levels first, and then I begin sinking through successive gradations of energy, going from the surface to the interior. As my mind moves through the music man's energy levels I can feel the emotions that are stuck in his energy field at different depths: anger, then fear, then sadness and despair. I've had this sense of sinking into energy fields when working with other patients, but never so vividly. Finally, plumbing the bottom, I have completely entered his internal environment. It's dark and scary, as if I were walking through a swamp. The music man seems to be comfortable with this type of energy work. He closes his eyes and relaxes, then takes a deep breath as I continue my journey through his inner world.

Walking through his internal swamp is frightening. The energy is dark, dank, and stifling. I move precariously through the mist, treading on soggy, unstable terrain. I know I'm standing in my office in Tucson, Arizona, but at the same time I'm somewhere else – another dimension, maybe, within my patient's inner reality? I sense something foreboding ahead, in the direction of my travel. It is dark, unpleasant, and sinister. I continue to move toward it in spite of its repugnance. I feel directed to investigate, almost compelled to do so. After a few minutes of inching nearer, I can tell that I'm very close to it, whatever it is. I have the sense that I can hear it breathing. I don't actually hear it with my ears, but I sense it breathing. It's a fantastical adventure where I know, that in a moment I'm going to confront this dark creature, and I don't know what will happen.

Suddenly, my patient raises his head and speaks. "By the way, I should tell you that I studied black magic with a shaman and I was given the lineage to carry...I don't want it anymore."

I wish he'd mentioned that before I blindly ventured into his dark, foreboding, and desperate inner world. Simultaneously with his statement, the entity raises its head from the murk of his inner swamp and I find myself face-to-face with the creature. It has a freakish, half-dog, half-baboon-shaped face and head. Scary, and what's scarier still, is that it is enormously powerful, far more powerful than I. It seizes me energetically. I cannot move. I am truly terrified. I feel that I'm in danger, not immediate physical danger, but another kind of danger, unlike any danger I have ever experienced. The creature doesn't like my intrusion. He knows that his dominion is being threatened, and he is not happy about it. I hear a voice in my head, but I am not initiating it. The voice – my own – is calling the name of Dr. Augosto from the Casa de Dom Ignacio. It seems strange to hear myself speak without having initiated the thought consciously. The response is immediate. I feel Dr. Augosto reach out through time and space as if an extra-dimensional portal has been opened. Using some force far greater than my own, he neutralizes the creature instantly. I am instructed without words to keep my energy where it is, to not retreat and to not move forward. I stay where I am, but I'm unable to see or feel exactly what is going on. I just wait and keep trying to energetically hold this extra-dimensional space so Dr. Augosto can do his work.

After five minutes, I am released, as if the energy that I was trying to hold onto just let go of me and dropped me from the music man's dark swamp back into my normal reality. Dr. Augosto is gone, the creature is gone, and the man from the music industry seems to be asleep. I am again standing in my treatment room in Tucson, Arizona. The sun is shining through the window, birds are chirping outside, and everything is normal: I am fully reintegrated back into my everyday reality. After the treatment, the music man thanks me and leaves.

I continue to have interesting although, thankfully, less dramatic insights while working with my patients over the following weeks. I begin to notice that many of my patients, maybe even most of them, have energetic blockages that relate to people they know. I call these blockages "attachments." An attachment occurs when a person's energy or a spirit's energy fastens to the spiritual fabric of another person causing a drag on the system that can manifest in any number of aberrations, emotional upset, low energy, codependency, even physical illness. Attachments can originate from almost anyone, usually from family members, spouses, ex-boyfriends, or ex- girlfriends. I still don't trust my sensibility completely, so I continue to ask my patients about what I find. It almost always makes sense to them when I describe the blockages I am finding. These attachments are always in relation to a person, an event, or a trauma. It can be an ex-lover who could never let go, a friend who is secretly jealous, or an angry business partner who feels slighted. The possibilities are endless, but the common thread among these attachments is some kind of unresolved emotion.

The worst attachments come from sexual predators. These attachments hang on tenaciously, believing they have some right to posses their victim, sometimes decades after the abuse. This really pisses me off. I strive to have compassion for people, but every time I run into one of these guys – and they are usually male, but not always – I find myself enjoying breaking the perpetrators' connection with their victims as much as I enjoy freeing the victims from the perpetrators. I can always defeat them. It's becoming my private war. I know I've still got some growing to do, but that's how it is for now.

People are coming to me more often for this other kind of work than for acupuncture. Sometimes people show up who don't even know I'm an acupuncturist. They just say, "My friend told me you could help me." When they find out I'm an acupuncturist they look confused, probably worried they're going to get poked with needles. I assure them that we can do the work without using needles. Only about half of my patients get acupuncture now. With many of them, I simply stand next to them with my hands hovered over their body taking in information and tuning their energy. It strikes me that the position I stand in now while working with people is the same position that Curt, the healer from Sedona, described when he saw the spirit of my grandfather standing at the end of the treatment table.

On the weekend Bunnie, Walt and I are returning from a delightful picnic high up in the Gates Pass foothills west of Tucson. As we walk past a small lookout area near the parking lot, I recognize the man from the music industry standing in a small crowd of locals and tourists. He spots me. I wave and say hello as he walks toward me. We chat briefly about some work he did with Steve Winwood, then he changes the subject to his treatment a few weeks earlier at the clinic. "You know that thing we did a few weeks ago? It worked. The old man died," he says, smiling.

89

"What old man?" I ask.

"My teacher, the black shaman, the witch doctor. He's dead," he says with a little smile that seems to indicate relief rather than grief. Wow! How do you respond to a man who tells you with a smile that his witch doctor teacher is dead?

"He is? That's interesting. Uh, how are you feeling?" I ask, not really knowing what to say.

"It's all good. I feel good. Thanks." He smiles and walks off to the viewing area.

Commentary from Spirit

Giving yourself over to dark energies whether out of curiosity, greed, quest for power, or for ego aggrandizement can lead you down a dark path where only the lucky escape unharmed. However, if you find yourself facing a sinister force more powerful than yourself, call in ernest for help. It will come.

Five Finger Meditation

Quote from Spirit

"Smooth your path. Walk with bare and tender feet. Discard the stones that bruise your tender flesh."
~Rayne

A Qigong master from China is visiting the university as a guest lecturer. He is here to share his knowledge, give lectures, and on the weekend, teach the Five Animal Frolics created by the legendary Chinese physician Hua Tou who lived in the second century AD. I received a call a few days ago to ask if I would help host him over the weekend. I agreed, and with some effort roused myself out of bed early on this sunny Saturday morning for the half-hour drive to the seminar in downtown Tucson

I drive into a rundown area of Tucson to find the seminar is being held in the basement classroom of a shabby, old building used as a youth center. I'm late, and it has already started when I walk through an open door to find fifteen or twenty people standing in a loosely- formed circle around an old Chinese man with bright eyes. The room has blue indoor-outdoor carpeting and a low ceiling with pipes crisscrossing in every direction. It shares the same aging paintwork as the rest of the building. The energy of the room is stagnant, dark, and oppressive – exactly the opposite of the little man in the center of the circle.

The old Chinese man smiles at me and motions for me to join the group. He is talking about how you can increase your health and well-being by following the natural movements of animals.

The Bear seems ponderous and slow, but he is powerful and determined. He likes water. Mimicking his movements will strengthen your kidneys, your bones, and your will. The old man bends his knees slightly and swings his arms and his torso from side to side in a slow lumbering motion. This is the first motion of the bear. Then he raises his hands like claws and with twinkling eyes makes a growling sound with an open mouth. This is the second motion of the bear. Everyone follows his movements and makes the growling sound, including me.

The Monkey is alert, agile, quick, and playful. He is thin but enormously strong. He uses a bent hand and wrist to grab branches. Following his movements will keep your mind nimble and your muscles strong. The old man bends his hands and wrists and pulls them close to his chest and gazes mischievously to the side, and then he allows his hands to open and relax as they move to his waist and his face becomes placid. This is the first movement of the monkey. Using the same hand position he steps forward, twists his torso, and stretches his arm forward with a swinging motion. Monkey reaches for fruit. This movement will help with digestion, he explains.

Everybody, including me, is enjoying the old man's playful nature. The exercises are gentle enough that even the older people in the group can do them, yet there are enough interesting movements to keep the younger people involved as well. I can see a depth of understanding within the old man that cannot be transmitted through these playful movements. His mind, his energy, and his body project an indefinable yet unmistakable subtlety that differentiates him from everyone else. I have seen the Five-Animal Frolics before, and I enjoy his presentation very much. He continues on.

The Deer is fast and supple. He has strong tendons and is gentle, but he will lock horns if necessary. If you move like a deer then you will strengthen the marrow and the spine, and calm your nerves. The old man makes the shape of horns by folding his middle and ring fingers down and extending the others. He bends his head down and stretches his hands and his spine forward, like a deer pushing his horns into an opponent. He retracts them, then steps forward on one foot and turns his head, torso, and his finger horns all at the same time to look behind himself. He does this on both sides.

After the third animal we break for lunch. I take the old man in my car, with the three university women hosting the seminar following in another car, and we drive to a Thai restaurant on Speedway. I soon learn that the university hosts were hoping I could show the old master around Tucson on Sunday. They can hardly understand the Chinese master's broken English, and they know nothing of Chinese culture or Chinese medicine. For the entire lunch hour the old master pays no attention to the women anyway. Though I have no idea what we would do on Sunday, I easily agree to do it. He is a nice enough guy. Maybe I can show him something he'll enjoy. The old master orders a vegetarian Thai salad and nothing to drink. During my years in Chinese medicine school and many lunches and dinners with subsequent Chinese medicine teachers, I have never seen any of them order raw food at a restaurant. The Chinese usually cook almost everything. They even braise lettuce, but he opts for a fresh veggie salad. I have Pad Thai and Thai iced tea. The tea is a huge mistake. Between the sugar and the caffeine I feel really hopped up. My heart is racing and I feel nervy, not the best for learning qigong. The conversation is sparse. I spend most of my time bouncing between the three women and the old master, trying to make everyone feel like they are not left out. That has probably been a mistake too, because I get stuck with the bill.

On the way back to the seminar, the old master sits in the passenger seat looking relaxed and content. I am on a caffeine and sugar rush and feel like driving a hundred miles an hour, but this is definitely not the place for it, so I chill out and attempt some conversation using my best Chinglish. I ask if he likes teaching Americans. He says they are different from the Chinese. They want to know everything up front, before they are ready, but they are enthusiastic. He likes to smile and have fun, so he enjoys teaching them.

Back in the dingy little basement suite the lessons resume. The Tiger is strong and fearless. He has sharp eyes and sharp claws. Following the movements of the tiger will build qi and expel disease from the energy meridians. The old master raises his hands toward the ceiling, and as he does this his spine seems to lengthen. He reaches up as high as possible then shapes his hands into claws as if he is clawing the sky and dragging it back down to Earth. He makes a loud hissing as he drags the sky downward. This is the first movement. Next he bends forward at the waist and reaches out with claw-like hands. The suppleness of his spine is at contrast to his advanced years. He bends easily and effortlessly. The rest of the group exhibits varying degrees of awkwardness.

The Crane flies through the air and gracefully dives to catch fish. If you move like the crane you will strengthen your heart and live a long life. The old master steps forward onto one foot while gracefully spreading his arms like wings. The first movement looks very much like ballet. This is flying. To dive, he steps out onto one foot and swings the opposite hand through the air in an arching motion down to the ground in front of him. He stands perfectly on one foot, completely bent at the waist, without wavering. The rest of the group is not as steady.

The old master explains that these exercises should be done every day and each one should be repeated three times. After one hundred days you will start to see benefits. And so ends the seminar.

*

Sunday morning I pick up the old master at his hotel. He is dressed in a pressed, green, short-sleeved shirt and khaki trousers pulled all the way up to his belly button, white socks, and brown leather shoes. He meets me with a broad smile on his face. He is obviously old, but his skin is smooth and supple, his body moves fluidly, and his eyes are bright and alert. We drive out east of Tucson to Saguaro National Park East where there is a huge cave system called Colossal Cave. We keep the top up and the air conditioning on. I don't want to fry the poor little guy in the Arizona sun. I pay five bucks at the tollbooth and then drive up to the parking lot where we get out. He stands with his heels together facing south and takes in a long slow breath. I can see his body grow an inch with his inhale. He does the same thing in all four compass directions, then raises his eyebrows and smiles at me.

We walk the short distance up to the cave entrance and pay another fee to get in. Just inside the air is immediately cooler. The cave temperature stays at about 70 degrees no matter what the outside temperature is. It is a welcome relief from the intense desert sun. We follow the guide as she escorts us through the maze of passages. We dutifully sit and listen, stand and admire, and try to keep up with the crowd. The docent explains that Apache Indians used to live in the cave, which is made of limestone, calcite, and gypsum, and that at least two people have died within it, both of them Native Americans, probably from the Apache nation. I'm not sure how much the old master understands, but at least he is being entertained. After a half-mile trek through stalagmites and stalactites, we emerge out of the cool earth into the blazing heat of southern Arizona. I ask the old master if he liked the tour. He said, "yes, very much." I don't think he got much out of it, actually, but at least he is polite.

"You doctor?" he asks.

"Yes, I am a Chinese doctor," I respond.

"Oh, Chinese doctor, not western doctor?" he asks. "Yes, I have a clinic here in Tucson."

"Oh, you have clinic in Tucson. You show me?" he asks. "Are you here on Monday?"

"No. Fly to Miami on Monday."

"Well, I can show you my clinic, but it's closed and I don't have any patients today," I tell him.

"Up to you," he replies.

"OK, why not, let's go," I say.

From Saguaro National Park East we take Old Spanish Trail to Speedway and then turn right on Kolb Road. Although many areas of Tucson combine beautiful desert with Mexican-adobe-inspired architecture, large swatches of the town are filled with flat, lifeless, cardboard-cutout houses built with the poorest materials and nothing but profit in mind. Unfortunately, much of the drive through east Tucson takes us through this lifeless wasteland of architectural mediocrity as we make our way toward the north side of Tucson. The old master stops observing the outside environment and turns his gaze inward. He places his hands on his lower abdomen and closes his eyes and smiles gently as we pass through east Tucson.

When we cross the bridge over the dry Rillito River the old master opens his eyes, which appear to be slightly glazed over and unfocused. Still smiling, he looks up at the Catalina Mountain range and traces the shape of the mountain ridge with his right forefinger. He nods approvingly. He becomes more alert as we turn left onto River Road. A few bends and gentle curves later we turn into the driveway. The gates swing open, and he studies the grounds as the tires crunch the pea-gravel driveway leading up to the house.

The old master repeats his ritual of facing the four compass directions and breathing deeply when we get out of the car. Upon finishing, he raises his eyebrows, smiles, and nods energetically. We walk to the front door. Before entering, he stops and looks at the Catalinas again and traces his finger over the ridge of the Santa Catalina Mountain range; he then continues with an S-like motion down to the point where we are standing in the front of the house.

"Dragon and Snake," he says. "Dragon and Little Dragon!" he says excitedly.

The old master looks at the terracotta fountain in the center of the foyer and then down the sixty-foot hallway. Whatever his thoughts are, he keeps them to himself. "My clinic is this way," I say. I show him to my treatment rooms. As he walks into my main treatment room his eyes are open, but he doesn't appear to be looking out of them. They are blank as if he is looking at the energy in the room and not at the material elements of the room. He touches his hand to my treatment table and closes his eyes for several seconds. The old master then opens his eyes and says, "OK." I have no idea what he means, but I assume the clinic tour is over, so I ask if he would like a cup of tea. He nods his approval.

I show him into the big airy room off the foyer. He sits comfortably in the lightweight wicker chair as I make the tea. I don't have Dr. Fuda's tea prowess, so we settle for green tea bags from Trader Joe's. The old master's eyes are closed again when I return to the room. When he opens them, he is not the smiling old man that I have become used to seeing. He looks stronger, more serious, and more intense. He looks at me, but not at my face. He looks at my chest.

"Yesterday you learn Five Animal dance. You know it already?" he continues to look at my chest as we speak. "I've learned it before, but with some different movements," I reply. I feel a tightening in my chest.

"In one day I could have told those students the secret of the Tao, but they would not be able to understand it. So, I showed them the Animal dance to open their meridians and to make them healthy. Do you understand this?" he says still gazing at my chest.

"Yes, I understand," I say. The tightness in my chest is getting more intense. I almost feel like crying. I can tell my lower lip is quivering.

"I can tell you the secret of the Tao in one sentence, but you will not understand what I say. The seven emotions are the internal root of disease. You use your hands and your qi to clear the seven emotions from your patients, yet you remain blocked within yourself. Therefore, you cannot understand the secret of the Tao. It is in front of you, but you cannot see it. You block yourself from the truth that is in front of you!" he says. I can feel my body buzzing inside as my chest continues to feel restricted.

"You are on a journey. I am not your true teacher, but I will teach you one thing, because you need to continue your journey and this will help you. You must clear the seven emotions from the five organs so you can connect your mind with your spirit. The way is simple." With that, he looks into my eyes and smiles, freeing my chest from his gaze. I feel the tension in my chest release immediately and I am able to take a deep breath.

"With the Five Finger Meditation you can clear emotions that block your heart, mind, and qi," he says. Then the old master shows me the step-by-step process to find and clear emotional blockages from the five energy systems. He says I must do this every day before working with patients.

"The Five Animal Dance is good for health and vitality, but the Five Finger Meditation is simpler, subtler, and deeper. It will clear emotional blockages and lead to spiritual awareness."

After the lesson his face resumes the kindly old-man look. Then he stands up and says, "I have to go to my hotel. I fly to Miami tomorrow."

He says nothing as I drive him to his lodging. At the hotel, I get out of the car, shake his hand with both of mine, bow my head, and say,

"thank you." He says, "OK, practice every day," and turns and walks spryly into the hotel.

92

Commentary from Spirit

You will overcome many barriers to spiritual ascendence on your journey. Most of them, if not all of them are within yourself. You always have a choice to fight your way through your blockages and suffer the trials and difficulties of doing so or to learn to remove your blockages, raise your energy and walk lightly on your path. It is up to you.

"One"

Quote from Spirit

*"The web of humanity connects every living soul. Touch one
and you touch all."*
~William

I feel the suffering of my patients. I feel their pain, their anger,
their sadness, and their despair. I am gaining a sense of compassion
that is true, immediate, and personal. Not only do I feel their
emotional suffering in my own body, but I can also locate it within
my patients' energy systems and clear it from them. I don't know
exactly how I am doing it, but it's working. These emotional
blockages are like magnetic structures. I can locate them with my
hands and my mind and then vibrate them out of their holding
place within the energy-structures of the patients' bodies.

I am also aware that I am taking on some of the emotional
blockages that I remove from my patients. Sometimes these
blockages disperse into the atmosphere, but often they instead land
on me. As a result, after a long clinic day I can find myself irritable,
angry, or just in a different mood. This transfer of emotions is not a
psychological phenomenon, but an energetic one. The energy of
blocked emotions has a near-physical structure that can move from
one person to another. People carry these structures around with
them and pass them onto others, who in turn may pass them onto
others still. I am starting to understand that the Five Finger
Meditation the old master taught to me is a method of identifying
and sequestering these energetic structures within my own body
and dissipating them. That's why I have to do it everyday before

clinic, so I don't pass these negative emotions onto my patients or onto anyone for that matter.

After using the Five Finger Meditation for several weeks, I can easily see how emotional blockages within my patients are related to other individuals. Past difficulties and traumas form an obstruction to the smooth flow of emotional energies. I'm beginning to understand how these blockages have stopped progress in certain areas of their lives. I can see, for instance, when a feeling of hurt has blocked someone from developing close relationships or how blocked anger has lead to chronic pain or disease. It is not difficult to use the meditation practice to dissipate the negative emotional structures that I pick up from my patients, as these blockages are new arrivals and do not connect deeply into my energy system.

However, it takes a great deal of concentration and focus to dissipate the negative emotional structures that come from my own personal experience, from my own trials and traumas. They are mine, my responsibility. I am becoming aware that these adverse structures are blocking my own personal and spiritual growth. They hold me down. Ultimately, they keep me from experiencing true spiritual love. They stop me from being a conduit of true spiritual love. Of course the old master could not give me his highest teachings, when he looked into my heart, he saw a closed door! Nothing in. Nothing out. I had walled myself off and I was spiritually bankrupt!

I thought I was so clever being able to see other peoples' emotional, energetic, and spiritual blockages, yet I was completely blind to my own. As I clear my own emotional blockages, am I also clarifying my own inner vision? Is this what the old master was talking about when he said the meditation will connect my mind with my spirit?

*

Clinic starts at 9AM on Monday morning. A middle-aged woman with grey-streaked hair sits in my treatment room chair. Her lips are pinched and her arms are folded tightly against her chest. I greet her and ask her to tell me why she is here. She has chronic digestive issues. I question her about diet and lifestyle – the usual. But, even before she speaks, I can see and feel her emotional blockages.

I hate coming to see doctors. I hate having this pain and bloating. A lot of people at work hate me and I think that has a lot to do with it. I've had this for a long time. I hate my mother. I think that's where it all started. I hated my family. I hated school. My childhood was terrible. I wasn't abused or anything, but I just hated it...

The blockage around her heart is like a concrete bunker. I cannot penetrate it. Even if I help her with her digestion, I will not be able to relieve her burden of hate. I can see that she came into the world with it. If she continues this way, she will leave the world with it. As she lies on the treatment table, I use the acupuncture points for her total condition – digestive, energetic, emotional. But her fortress is strong. It will not break. She must open the gates herself, and it is not her time – she is not ready. She is committed to her stronghold and to her hate. It's so sad to see. She has blinded herself with hatred and locked herself away from her own progress and growth. She has locked herself away from love.

*

I don't miss a day of the Five Finger Meditation. Even if I can only do it for two minutes, I do it. Every day I slough off some more of my own blockages. It's always incomplete and I sometimes feel like I am going backward, but I continue on.

I have also been practicing Three Lines qigong before bed to help me sleep. It's a type of progressive relaxation that also gently replenishes energy. I fall asleep easily tonight, as if I am gently being taken away on a floating cloud, but I soon wake up with a start. I am not in my bed. I am in an operating room. Though I have no sense of smell, I can see, hear, and feel. I do not have any fear. I am completely conscious and not dreaming. I cannot see the surgeons, but I can feel their presence. Kind and reassuring, the surgeons are in the form of light. My sternum is being cut down the middle and my rib cage is being opened. I begin to feel pain and fear, but it is far removed and cannot touch me, as if I am under anesthesia, yet I am completely conscious at the same time. One of the surgeons reaches into my chest. I feel him doing something to my heart, and then my consciousness is removed completely. I feel and see nothing. There is no time, no sensation – just emptiness. I am nowhere. I am blank. I exist in a void. I am the void.

After an indeterminable amount of time – that is, if there is such a thing as time here – my consciousness returns. I am in a hospital bed. There is a nurse whom I can almost see directly. She is made of light, but it's not as bright as that of the surgeons. I know her, and she knows me. We have known each other for a long time. We are in love, but it has been a very long time since I have seen her. She is close to me and I want to touch her, but when I move, I can feel my separated chest bones move against each other where my sternum has been repaired. The whole area feels extremely vulnerable. My chest has been surgically closed, but my heart has been opened. I stay in the hospital bed for several days. My nurse, my love from another spiritual reality, stays by my side. Even in my hospital bed in this other dimension, I can see that she too has blockages. She is imperfect as am I. I can feel her being. She is putting off her own spiritual growth in order to help me grow. I don't know how I know this, but I know. Soon, I am told that I have recovered enough to return. But I don't want to go. I am at peace here. I am loved in a way that I have not known before – spiritual love. I want to ask if I can stay, but it's too late. I am back in my bed in Tucson.

My eyes open. It is dark. I don't think any time has passed since I closed my eyes to go to sleep. I still feel like my chest is vulnerable and I shouldn't move, but as I feel around with my hand, I can tell everything is intact. What I just experienced wasn't a dream – it was reality. Now, here in Tucson, in my bedroom, this physical existence is only itself a dream. I close my eyes again, and this time fall into a deep sleep. Again, I am transported to another dimension, and I am not dreaming, but traveling. Someone, whom I cannot see, is carrying me through space independent of the passage of time. I am flying thousands of miles over the surface of the Earth, but no time is going by. All at once, yet in a relaxed sequence, I am shown things that I don't want to see. I see starving children in Africa. I see men toiling in fields in South East Asia. But I don't just see the men toiling. At the same time I feel their pain, their anguish. I feel their family's distress. I see those who are inflicting suffering upon them, and I see the pain of the perpetrators as well. I am moved to Eastern Europe where I see strong young men with missing limbs from battle injuries. In America, I see emotional strife at home. I can't take any more. It's too much. I force myself back into my bed in Tucson and open my eyes. I awaken, but the vision does not stop and the images keep coming; not only images, but entire holographic imprints including emotions, suffering, and events that relate to the suffering.

I get out of bed and walk into the living room and look around at the walls and the furniture. I touch things, the wall, the chair, the floor. I am here. I am awake. But the vision still goes on. I fall to the floor in a heap. I can hear myself wailing, tears are falling from my eyes, but it still doesn't stop. Over and over I am shown suffering in the world. I don't have enough strength in my physical body or in my mind to stop the relentless sequence of suffering. Europe, Africa, Asia, America, example after example of the suffering of humanity. And it's not only happening faster and faster; it's happening all at the same time. Worse, yet, I see and feel each and every experience of individual suffering as if it were my own. I cannot fight it. I am broken and it still does not stop.

As I lie on the floor sobbing, I hear a loud yet gentle, and enormously powerful voice – ONE. "ONE," it says. The images begin to fade. "One" – the voice booms in my ears. What does it mean? I am one? It only takes one person do make a difference? "One," the voice rings. We are all one? "One." The voice stops. The images stop. I am by myself in my living room. I have nothing left – no energy, no strength. I can barely lift myself off the floor. I wipe the tears from my face and drag myself back into the bedroom. I crawl into bed and fall into a quiet slumber.

Commentary from Spirit

From the heart, you communicate with all of humanity, touching one person individually, then all of humanity through the interconnections made from one heart to another. To close off you heart is to close yourself off from humanity. To open your heart is to lift humanity on wings of light.
Find your fear, anger, and hurt. Cast it out and open your heart.

www.MichaelRoland.com

Doctor, Doctor

Quote from Spirit

"We speak to you. Hear our words. We guide you. Accept our guidance. We send to you the Great Healing Light. Open your heart and take it in."
~Rayne.

Dr. Evan Kligman is a super achiever. And, he is a nice guy. He had been a Professor and Head of a Department of Family and Community Medicine and is currently in private practice in Tucson. He also is medical director of an inpatient hospice unit and free clinic when he is not studying theology or writing medical papers. Today, he is in my treatment room. He is pale, apprehensive, and frail – he doesn't look good. He has an abnormal heart rhythm called atrial fibrillation. The cardiologists at Pima Heart will give him a full cardiac workup, and he should have results by next week. I have treated Evan before for minor complaints. Today, things are different.

I take Evan's pulse in the traditional style of Chinese medicine – three fingers on each wrist. His heartbeat is rapid, and his pulse is weak and thready. I can feel panic and fear in his energy. I insert the acupuncture needles in his arms and legs and then begin to move deeper into his energy field using my own form of qigong energy work. I sink gently through layers of tension in Evan's energy field until I find his heart, which has its own type of tension associated with it. I can feel the energy of the heart muscle and the nerves connected to it. His heart is busy, focused, working, and rying to keep pace, but it is failing. My energy moves to other tructures surrounding his heart - his aorta, his sternum, his rib cage. I feel the tissues relax with the acupuncture and energy work, but his heart still maintains the same energetic tension. I don't think I can help him very much. There has to be some intervention beyond me if there is going to be a big change for the better.

After the treatment Evan is relaxed. There is color in his face and he looks a little more vibrant, but he still carries apprehension. I would, too, if I were waiting to find out my fate from the cardiologists. I ask him to make an appointment with Bunnie for a spiritual treatment. Her spiritual work often relieves fear and anxiety, and sometimes other more interesting things happen as well. Evan agrees to come back after he gets his results. We say goodbye for now.

I feel a sense of inadequacy that often accompanies my failure to help a friend suffering with a medical or energetic issue. Every day I live and die by my successes and failures. I imagine that some day I will break this up and down cycle, but for now it is with me. It drives me. I know deep down that it also holds me back. What would happen if I let go of this emotional attachment to results? What would happen if I were able to accept my own failings and the failings of others? Thankfully, I have a busy clinic schedule today, so I won't have to contemplate this question for long.

Three Postdoctoral Fellows from the university are here to shadow me on my rounds. They are all young. There is a man with glasses and that too-intelligent-for-his-own-good look, an attractive woman with deep brown eyes and dark hair, and a good-natured blond girl with a bobbed haircut. These are all experienced doctors who are returning as students and taking additional training in alternative medicine. They are interested, eager, and respectful.

The first patient we see together is a middle-aged woman with long, dry, graying hair. She looks frightened and desperate. I have seen her before, but these docs have not. Her left hand is wrapped in a worn bandage that looks like it has been on and off a hundred times. When she unwraps her hand, it looks normal apart from the marks from the bandages, but she has intense nerve pain, numbness, tingling, and burning. The worst pain is in her thumb. She takes multiple doses of narcotics daily to try to control it, but the drugs have negative side effects of drowsiness, lethargy, and addiction.

I don't need to ask any questions or take her pulses. This is simple: pain in thumb. With the docs quietly standing around the table, I select a thin acupuncture needle and insert it obliquely into her right big toe. I sense her pain evaporate instantly. She confirms this, verbaly. The docs look at each other and smile. Outside the treatment room the young docs ask how I was able to select the point that would make the pain disappear instantly. "Chinese medical theory told me where to place the needle, but the exact position was determined by the emotional energy stuck in that point and in the area of the pain," I explain, only to see blank faces all around.

"Chinese meridian theory tells me that the pain in one part of the body will respond to needling in another part of the body that is related by the meridian system, the system of energy pathways. But it was my energetic palpation of the restricted emotions related to the condition that guided my final placement of the needle to yield instant results," I say, starting to feel very doctorial and clever.

"So, it was all in her head," responded the brainy one.

"No. It was in her thumb," I say with a smile.

"I mean it is psychosomatic. She thinks she has pain, therefore she has pain," he quipped.

"Are you suggesting that her miraculous powers of thought also created positive findings on a nerve conduction test?" I respond. He didn't know about the medical tests, but I couldn't help myself.

"Oh, I was going to ask you about that," he smiles. The other two smile as well. "If her nerve pain is real, then why did one small needle in her toe stop it so fast and so completely? There aren't any nervous connections between her right toe and left thumb," he says.

"Thoughts are real. Emotions are real. Pain is real. In this case she has positive findings in a nerve conduction test as well. Those are real, too. The reason the needle in her toe stopped her pain is because it interrupted the pain signal on an energetic level. As you say, there are no nervous connections between the right toe and the left thumb – but there are energetic relationships. More importantly, the needle dispersed the emotional blockage that relates to her pain. No blockage, no pain."

The young doctors look thoughtful for a moment. I am reminded of my teachers and an old saying in Chinese medicine. Tong zi bu tong, bu tong zi tong. It means: Where there is blockage, there is pain. Where there is no blockage, there is no pain.

"How were you able to assess that there is an emotional blockage, and how did you know exactly where it was?" asks the astute, dark- haired woman.

"The emotional blockage, I can feel through her energy. The exact location of the blockage is not in any physical reality, but it affects her physical reality. So, in this case, I located the acupuncture point using Chinese medicine theory, then I placed the needle at the precise angle and depth by feeling her emotional energy that was stuck at that point. I allowed that stuck emotional energy to guide the depth and angle of insertion," I explain to her. The doctors go quiet, so I take the moment to go back and check on my patient.

Tears are streaming from her eyes as I enter the room. She says the pain has come back. I adjust the placement of the needle a fraction of a millimeter, and the pain disappears and she stops crying. Holding my hands about a foot-and-a-half over her abdomen, I can feel her pain – not her nerve pain, but her emotional pain. Her emotions and her energy are in chaos, desperately seeking order, but not having any stable reference to judge what order might look like. My intrusion into this energetic and emotional chaos causes further turmoil – her body begins to convulse and her breath quickens. She begins to scream out loud in rhythm with the convulsions. However, she is not in pain. She is experiencing a somatic manifestation of the imbalanced energy in her body. The manifestation has been brought on because the intrusion of my relatively stable energy has called attention to her internal chaos. I tell her that she is safe and, with her permission, we should continue this process until it finishes. She nods in agreement. Her body continues to convulse as I focus more intently on her energy.

I flow with the chaotic pattern of her energy like a stick floating in a violent river. I am being tossed about on waves of chaos, but soon I am able to guide some of her energy. With subtle yet firm guidance my steady energy begins to influence her raging river of chaotic energy. After a few minutes, I am able to guide her energy completely. My energy then becomes the river, and her energy becomes the stick. I calm my energy to the point that her energy can float on it peacefully like a stick floating on a quiet lake. Her body stops convulsing, her breath slows, her arms fall to her sides, and I can see a smile forming on her face. I gently remove my energy from hers and allow her to rest quietly until the acupuncture needle is removed.

The Fellows continue to follow me until lunchtime and then go on their way. The rest of the day is easy and I am able to finish by 5PM. However, by day's end I feel surrounded by a miasma of discordant energy. It is weighing me down as if I were carrying a heavy load. I feel anger, sadness, and irritability creeping in and trying to affect my emotions. Some time ago, I would have thought these to be my emotions, my energy. Now, I know they are energetic structures from patients; and the structures have attached themselves to me during my work. Though they are attached to me, I will not take them on as my own. I can dissipate the attachments by doing the Five Finger Meditation. If I practice the meditation first thing in the morning and first thing after work, I am able to keep my energy clean and free of unwanted hangers-on.

The next morning Bunnie hands me my patient files and tells me that I have a new client, the daughter of an important doctor. It must be my week for doctors! When I enter the treatment room, I find a 20-year-old blond girl who is pretty, but too thin and obviously troubled. Her mother and father are also in the room.

"Hi, I'm Michael," I say upon entering the room.

"I'm Doctor Michael Pearlman. This is my wife, Sarah, and my daughter, Michelle. I want to be very clear with you. Before I retired, I was the Chief of Psychology and Geriatrics at the university medical center. I am a scientist and a physician. I'm not here because I believe in what you do. I'm here, frankly, because it is our last resort," says Doctor Important. Well, that's an impressive opening line. "My daughter has an eating disorder that no one can help with. I have diagnosed her with post-traumatic stress disorder. I believe it to be the cause of her anorexia nervosa," continues the doctor.

"Well, let's see what we can do," I say. With one glance, I can see that the problem is all in her head. I don't mean she is making it up – I mean the energy causing the problem is stuck mainly in the region of her head. I ask her if she would like to get onto the treatment table.

When she is on the table lying in front of me, I slip my hands underneath her head and ask her to relax. I can immediately feel the tension of her energy blockage. Within seconds she begins to cry.

"What are you doing?" inquires the doctor.

"It's OK, daddy," responds his daughter.

Her crying stops and starts several times during the treatment session, and then suddenly she begins to laugh. I laugh. Even her parents laugh. With the session completed, I say, "OK, let's do three treatments in a row and see what happens."

"So, we should schedule in your front office?" he asks.

"That would be great," I say.

The next day the doctor and his daughter come in, without the mother. When I enter the treatment room the doctor looks hostile. He says, "I don't believe it." His daughter is smiling.

"You don't believe what?" I ask.

"You just cured anorexia nervosa in one treatment! And that can't be done. However, my daughter has been suffering with this for over a year, and now it's gone. I have been with my daughter non-stop, and the only intervention she has had recently has been your treatment. That leads me to a conclusion that I am not comfortable with," he says.

What a bizarre perspective. No wonder his daughter is so messed up. I'm really not sure how to handle his aggressive compliment.

"That's fantastic! Let's follow through with our three treatments and then reassess," I say.

"I'd like to make an appointment for myself as well," says the good doctor.

"I'd be happy to work with you Dr. Pearlman," I respond.

"Call me Michael," he says. I finish treatments with Michelle and then continue to work with Michael periodically over the next several months.

It's been an eventful week in the clinic, and I am happy when the weekend rolls around. Bunnie has a cabin on Mount Lemmon. She sometimes invites a group of friends on the weekend.

This weekend she's invited our mutual friends, Oswald and his wife, Sherri. It gets cold at night eight thousand feet above the desert. Bunnie asks me to light a fire in the rustic, hand-laid stone fireplace. We all sit around watching the dance of the flame and enjoying the popping, crackling, and sizzling of the wood. For the first time, I notice how much Oswald looks like a mountain man. Not a fat, hairy type of mountain man, but more of a mythical steward-of-the-woods and friend-to-the-animals type of mountain man. Bunnie makes him a cup of hot chocolate with Jamaican rum. Oswald sits in his chair in front of the fire like he has been there for ages, his tall, thin frame folded into a form of contentment with both hands wrapped around his warm mug.

Seeing him sit there in a moment of bliss strikes mixed chords within me. I am happy to see my friend contented; I have never seen him this way before. Yet it makes me realize that I am far from contented even though my life is good and I have every reason to be so. As the fire dies down, we all sleep peacefully in the little mountain hideaway.

The next morning we enjoy a long walk around the loop of cabins followed by breakfast on the deck. It's a perfect mountain morning. The air is crisp, the sky is clear, and the smell of pine trees wafts across the deck. Birds chirp away and squirrels play in the trees as we eat our breakfast and enjoy the company of friends.

When I return to clinic on Monday morning, I see Dr. Kligman in the waiting room and stop to chat with him before his spiritual session with Bunnie. He has always been bright, energetic, and positive. But today he looks pale, fatigued, and frightened. I am still worried about him. The results are in from his cardiac workup.

He has brought along a friend, a surgeon, and they have been discussing heart procedures. Dr. Kligman explains that he has been diagnosed with a heart condition that will require open-heart surgery to replace one of his valves. From here on out he will become weaker and weaker until he gets the operation or dies from heart failure. There are no other options. Tucson has excellent cardiologists, surgeons, and heart treatment centers. However, Cleveland Clinic in Cleveland, Ohio, is the best for the operation that Evan needs. He is a doctor and he knows the risks.

In a fit of blatant optimism I say, "Well, let's just get you better so you won't have to worry about that!" He looks at me kindly and nods his head as he smiles. I don't know if he is thinking that I am being kind, ignorant, and optimistic or that I am just plain stupid. I feel kind of uncomfortable after I say it. I know his condition isn't going to be fixed by my energy work. The face of Evan's surgeon friend has an amiable, but nevertheless condescending expression toward me. Feeling really stupid, I tell Evan to enjoy his session with Bunnie, and I exit for a treatment room and my first patient of the day.

After a few minutes, I hear Evan and Bunnie beginning their session in the neighboring treatment room. I can't hear the words they are saying, but I can hear the murmur of words being spoken. Within minutes of beginning the treatment with my patient, I sense a huge amount of energy forming in Bunnie's room. The energy is powerful enough to distract me from my work. Normally, I can focus like a laser, but the energy in the other room is increasing every minute. I force myself to focus on my patient, but I still have to split my attention because I cannot ignore what is happening in the other room.

I am standing at the side of my treatment table doing energy work on my patient, who is relaxed with her eyes closed, as I feel the energy in the other room building to a crescendo. Just when I think it is about to peak and diminish, it holds steady, and stays at a high level of intensity. As I continue to work on my patient, the magnitude of the energy in the next room compels me to look in its direction. I blink several times to make sure I am seeing what I am seeing: a swirling, white vortex is forming on the wall between our rooms. As I watch, a translucent figure in white walks through the wall. He is just over five feet tall and probably about 110 or 120 pounds, but of course he doesn't weigh anything – he is made of light. He is completely translucent and has no legs, just a torso with arms and a head. His lower body fades into clear light. He has a well-trimmed beard and mustache and he wears a suit that probably comes from the 19th century. He knows I can see him, but he walks right through me anyway. My body shudders as he passes through it. I turn around and find him on the other side of my treatment table where he appears to be assessing my patient. I keep looking at him to make sure I'm not just imagining things, but his image persists. Suddenly, I feel an overwhelming sense of loving acceptance. I feel like a child and he is like a father and mother at the same time. Without words he tells me that he is a surgeon, and then he places my hands above my patient in a particular position. I feel energy move through my hands.

The translucent surgeon stands behind me now. Without warning, he walks directly into my body. Immediately, I feel light-headed. My lips begin to try to form words that are not my own, but my throat tightens to stop them. I feel like I am going to choke. I think I am going to pass out, so I step back with my right foot to catch myself then he instantly releases me. My head clears and my throat relaxes, but he is still close by, standing behind me again. He puts a message into my head to tell my patient and then disappears.

I finish treating my patient and am about to leave the room, but the message keeps banging away inside my head. Unable to contain myself, I blurt out, "Your son is going to be OK."

She looks at me incredulously and says, "Thank you." Then she looks up to her left, cocks her head, and beams a smile at me, "Thank you very much!"

Some weeks go by before I see Evan again. When he comes in for treatment, he looks markedly better.

"Have you had your operation already? You went to the Cleveland Clinic, right?" I ask. "Yes, I went to Cleveland, but they sent me home," he says. "What?! What do you mean?" I ask. This is interesting.

"Well, I got there. They restudied my heart valve by repeating a 2D echo and a stress echo, and noticed improvement in the regurgitation of blood. The night before the scheduled surgery, the surgeon told me "Go home. You don't need an operation!" he said with a big smile.

I don't know exactly what happened in Bunnie's treatment room or how the spirit surgeon might have affected the progress of Evan's heart condition. But, being in the direct presence of the spirit surgeon and hearing of Evan's incredible recovery have left me humbled, grateful, and curious about the possibilities.

Commentary from Spirit

Kind beings are always working on your behalf. They are always trying to be heard, always trying to offer guidance, and always trying to help you. It is not up to you to become a psychic or a seer, but learn to open your mind to let thoughts, ideas, help, and healing come to you. They may be received by you as your own thoughts and ideas, but it doesn't matter, higher spirits do not need to get credit, but they have a great desire to be of service.

Reality of Spirituality

Quote from Spirit
"Your journey is long. Your stay here is short."
~I Lin

A spirit surgeon walking through the wall into my treatment room, Dr. Augusto stretching his long, invisible arm from above to protect me from the witch doctor, colored lights dropping out of the ceiling into my patients, the souls of little, fluffy, four-legged creatures jumping out of their bodies in front of me, and all the other experiences of the past few years have led me to wonder what's really going on in the spirit world that is hidden beyond our normal everyday perceptions. What is the spirit world like and how does it work? Bunnie spent 15 years in Sao Paulo, Brazil, where she worked with the spiritist community there. I ask her what she thinks is really going on in the nonphysical world.

"I'm not an expert. I was just a tiny, little, insignificant part of the spiritist group in Brazil," Bunnie responded. I don't believe her for a minute. I've known Bunnie for two years now; she is the most honest person I've ever met in my entire lifetime. She is also, sometimes, modest beyond reason. So I press her, saying, "It's just that I'm getting a lot of information in regard to things spiritual and I'm trying to figure out how it all works."

Bunnie gives me a penetrating look and says, "I spent a long time working with my group in Brazil. At first, I didn't understand or believe the things they were saying. I was only there at the invitation of my equitation master, who was a famous Olympian and colonel in the Brazilian army. Nobody disobeyed the colonel, especially me. So I did as I was told to do. I attended the meetings just to please him. At first, I didn't believe anything they had to say. As my understanding grew, the things they were saying began to make sense. The leader of our group was a chief justice in Brazil. He was very thorough and made sure the people in the group developed their sense of observation and reason over their sense of imagination and emotion. It was several years before I got a complete picture of how things work."

Over the next several months Bunnie and I have long, in-depth discussions on spirituality and the nature of spiritual reality. I realize that I have never had a well-formed understanding or even a belief system that included a spiritual reality. When I was younger I dismissed the notion of God and heaven. I based my uninformed opinion on the thought that if there really were a God he wouldn't allow so much pain and suffering. That was a bit juvenile, I admit, but then I was a juvenile. Later, I dismissed religion, based on the hypocrisy I saw in some religious people – another hasty conclusion. As I grew into adulthood I began to adopt the "random chance" philosophy, which goes something like: we sprang up by random chance from some primordial soup, evolved into amoebae, and then participated in a Darwinian transformation into humans, who live their lives and then cease to exist. As I grew older, I decided it was likely that we don't cease to exist completely when we die, but rather that we cease to be who we are. We lose our individuality, and our consciousness disperses into some kind of greater consciousness. This last of my theories has hung uneasily in the background of my consciousness for the past ten years as a likely, but unsubstantiated, reality.

Now, in the light of new experiences, I am faced with the necessity to reevaluate my poorly conceived theories. The more I talk with Bunnie about spiritual reality and how the spirit world works, the more my recent spiritual experiences start to make sense, especially with my acceptance of two large concepts: the afterlife and reincarnation.

The concept of the afterlife – continued consciousness after death – was something I could not accept for most of my life because I have always relied on direct experience over faith, much to the chagrin of those few religious friends I have had. However, over the last couple of years I have had multiple encounters with nonphysical beings in my clinical work. Seeing these spiritual beings with my own eyes, feeling the energetic effects of their presence and their work, and witnessing the resulting improvements in patient's conditions provided the direct experience that allowed me to accept the actuality of the afterlife.

Reincarnation is the second concept necessary to understand spiritual reality. Both reincarnation and the existence of an afterlife are consistent with many religious beliefs around the world. In Western religion, however, the notion of reincarnation is largely disregarded, and it is commonly believed that after one (and only one) lifetime we die and go directly to heaven or, possibly, to hell. I have to admit this has always bothered me. Not just the heaven and hell thing, but the whole idea that one lifetime – just one tiny time-span of action and consciousness – can lead to an eternity of bliss or eternal suffering. Relative to eternity our lifetimes are short, finite, and virtually insignificant. Do our few good deeds in this one lifetime afford us an everlasting audience with God? Do our sins, however bad, merit everlasting suffering in the fires of hell for eternity? For many in the West, the denial of even the possibility of reincarnation can be a big sticking point that blocks many from considering the idea of an eternally evolving spiritual reality.

What really happens after we die? I pose the question to Bunnie.

"In our spirit group we learned that life on earth is like going to school. There are experiences to be had, friends to be made, and lessons to be learned. At the end of our term we are evaluated, and then we go home, to our real home, our spiritual home. There we find ourselves in the loving company of our spiritual family. We have clarity and we can review our lifetime and consider our actions. At some point it is decided that we must return back to school for our next term. As we are born into a new lifetime to begin our new term at school, we try to use the lessons we have learned in our last lifetime to continue our progress," she said.

"Okay, you're saying that life on Earth is like school. At the end of our life we get evaluated and then we go home. Home is where we live in the spirit world with our spirit family. While we're at home with our spirit family, we consider all the things we did on Earth and what we've learned from them. Then, when it's time to go back, we apply what we've learned to our next lifetime. Is that right?" I ask.

"Yes, we go home to the true reality." "Is that what you believe?"
"Yes."
"So, you believe in reincarnation?"

"Without reincarnation we wouldn't have the chance to correct our mistakes and to continue our growth and learning as spirits. Our spiritual evolution would stop at the moment we died. Instead, we are allowed to return to Earth to rectify the wrongs we have committed and to learn lessons that will allow us to evolve as spirits."

"Does that mean we just keep returning lifetime after lifetime on into eternity?"

"We return as many times as needed in order to learn our lessons."
"How many times is that?"
"For most people it is many lifetimes."
"Oh, so, there is an end to it. What happens after that?"

"When we have learned our spiritual lessons then we have a choice to come back to earth to help others or to remain in our spiritual home, but that choice comes only after many lifetimes," she says.

"So, if we learn these lessons, we graduate from the cycle of living earthly lives and dying earthly deaths, and then get to stay in the spirit world?"

"Yes, unless you choose to come back to help others to learn their lessons – but it's your decision at that point."

"What are these lessons we have to learn?"

"They are things like love, compassion, kindness, and learning to be fair, just, and unselfish."

I remember the overwhelming sense of loving acceptance from the spirit surgeon who visited my treatment room. He must have perfected his expression of loving acceptance over many lifetimes to such a degree that it radiates out from his being. Just standing in his presence was enough to become engulfed in the sensation. I don't think that's what everyone feels when I walk into a room. I must have a long way to go.

"So, the idea is that we keep getting better and better at being compassionate, loving, and so on until we graduate from Earth school?"

"Yes."

"Okay. If everyone is here trying to learn how to become good, then why are people so bad to each other?" In asking this question I feel like a child. Why are people bad? Why is the sky blue? As rudimentary as this question is, it has truly puzzled me throughout my lifetime.

"Everyone comes to Earth for the first time not knowing these things. They have to be here to learn the lessons that will allow them to grow into higher spirits," Bunnie says.

"Then why aren't we just told from the beginning what we are supposed to be doing here?" I ask.

"There are reasons beyond our understanding why things are hidden from us, but the basic values are readily available to anyone to learn. We have to exercise our free will and choose to learn them."

"What if we don't?" Obviously, many people don't bother with kindness, generosity, and compassion.

"If we don't, then we keep repeating lifetimes until we do. But if we continue to resist learning our lessons, they keep getting more unpleasant until we finally decide to get it right."

"So, we're punished for being bad?" I ask, again feeling like a child.

"We are helped to see the right way."

"Why should we have to suffer? What good does it do? If, like you say, we come down here to learn our lessons, how to be kind and unselfish, then why do we have to go through so much pain? I mean, how do war and disease and personal suffering fit into it? Couldn't we learn the things that we are supposed to learn without so much pain and suffering?"

"The question of suffering is a hard one. The leader of our spirit group in Brazil used to say that each of us is like a precious stone mined from the earth. We have to suffer cutting and polishing before we can become a jewel."

Another sense I had felt in the presence of the spirit surgeon was that of being a child and him the parent. I doubt he was really my spirit parent or anything like that, but the difference between us was so great that I felt like a child in his presence. Maybe I am a child in spirit and he is an adult in spirit. We often find it easy to show love and acceptance toward a baby who is so much smaller and so much more vulnerable than us. Is that how higher spirits see us? Do they see us as children whose seemingly difficult trials are merely learning experiences, even though we, ourselves, experience our trials as serious and painful events?

Commentary from Spirit

This temporal existence is one you many you will have and have had. Your time on earth is short, but there is much to do. Make the most of what is available to you. Learn and grow. Free yourself to be as a child at school, eager to absorb, expand, and mature.

Casting Out Carlos

Quote from Spirit

"You are a child. I will hold your hand. I am great. You are small. Take comfort that I will look after you."
~The Angel

One of my patients, Esmerelda a short dark haired woman with deep brown eyes, drives in from New Mexico once a month for a treatment. She has over thirty years of training and practice in Native American traditions, Reiki energy work, yoga, and shamanism. Esmerelda has a long laundry list of symptoms and complaints mostly stemming from a genetic disorder. The doctors have diagnosed her, but they can't do anything for her. Her case is complicated and I must be very careful and focused when I work with her. If I make any miscalculations with my acupuncture needle formula, not only would it not help her, but it could take her weeks just to recover. Over several months I have developed a good relationship with her. She has a deep knowledge of energy medicine, and she trusts me to do the right thing for her. I don't take her trust lightly.

Heart palpitations, migraine, restriction in the throat, joint pain, numbness of the limbs, and insomnia are on the menu today for Esmerelda. However, after treating her several times, I've stopped listening to her list of symptoms. It's not that I don't believe her or I'm not interested. It's because her problems are so deeply rooted that the symptoms are far removed from the underlying issues. Only her pulses and her energy can tell me what I need to know. I take her pulse in the Chinese way, three fingers on both wrists and then look at her energy. To read her energy I extend my hands, palm down, about eighteen inches above her body, one above her chest, one above her abdomen. Her energy is calm and weak. I expected weak, but it should be chaotic and confused, based on her poor health, not calm.

I am very careful with her – too much energy work could send her into a tailspin taking weeks in bed to recover from. So I take my time and proceed gently. As I continue to hold my hand above her body I'm being drawn deeper into her system, deeper than I want to go. She knows all about energy work, so I can tell her what is going on and she will understand.

"I'm having to go pretty deep today, is that OK?"

"You have to do something, I can't go on like this. I'm just getting worse and worse."

"OK, I'm going to go slowly." I say.

"What's that?" she asks. She felt it before I did.

"Um, I don't know yet. Give me a minute...Oh!"

"What is it? What do you feel?" she asks.

"Just a minute. Let me lock onto it. There's someone hooked in here."

"I know who it is."

"OK, well, whoever it is they have been here for a while. He's male, I'm sure of that."

"I know who it is," she said with certainty.

"Give me just a minute to sequester his energy. Then say his name and I'll be able to tell if we are onto the right person...OK, say his name, please."

"Carlos."

"No, nothing. This is someone else's energy," I respond. "I'm sure it's him."

"Say his name again."

"Carlos."

"No, nothing. There's no response from this energy pattern, it must be someone else."

"Joe Cortez."

"Whoa, that's him! Wow, is he strong!" A huge burst of energy vibrates my body. I am almost thrown back against the wall, but I maintain composure. The energy pattern that I had isolated is now buzzing and pulsating.

"Yes, that's his other name. I knew it was him. I've never been able to get clear from him."

"An old boyfriend?"

"Yes, you could say that, but there's a lot more to it. I can't really talk about it. The witches from the coven are still around. I think they still want to get me."

I think we just stepped out of my realm of experience. Witches, coven? Why not? I'm getting to the point where I don't disbelieve anything out of hand. I wait and see.

"Are you worried about these witches?" I ask.

"They've always been out to get me. I met Carlos in New Mexico a long time ago. We were lovers, but I never joined his group of women. They were all jealous."

"So, this guy was famous? Was he a rock star or something?"

"He might as well have been. Carlos wasn't his only name."

Mmmpff, that hurt: a sudden jolt, just like a sock in the gut, travels through my arm and into my midsection. I'd better stay on my toes.

"His other name was Joe Cortez." 126

At the utterance of this name, I feel the energy that I am locked onto kick and jump like a baby moving in his mother's womb. I take a few minutes to work with the energy belonging to Joe Cortez. His conscious energy is here within her, and he is starting to recognize that I am here as well. I can feel it. He knows I am interfering and he doesn't like it. But before I can remove this energy from my patient, I have to sequester it completely. I have had this sense of a conscious entity being deeply attached to a patient before with other work I have done, but it has never been so immediate, so present, and so alert. I can feel the energy around me starting to ramp up. The room begins to pulsate with an electromagnetic charge. My skin tingles and my pores open with sweat as waves of energy permeate my body.

"This is getting pretty intense. Are you up for this?" I ask.

"I've got to do it. I've been trying for years to move his energy out, but I can't do it. I need help."

"OK, let's see what we can do."

Joe Cortez holds a personal energy pattern within the surrounding energy of my patient. I am able to identify his energy and differentiate it from hers – this is the first part of taking it out. It's like removing a tumor. I have to cut away all the connections before I remove it. But this isn't a tumor – it's a consciousness and he knows I'm here. The energy in the room continues to build and pulsate, it's preparing for something. My body is beginning to feel like it is more energy than it is physical. I am losing the perception of physical boundaries. My energy is extending into and merging with the growing energy within the room. My physical and energetic boundaries feel vague. I begin to lift out the energy of Joe Cortez from the surrounding energy of my patient. And, oh...but no. I can't. As soon as I try to lift his energy out, it becomes heavy and immovable. He is stronger than me. I can't move him. Meanwhile, the energy in the room continues to build.

"Can you feel that?" I ask.

"He's very strong."

"Yes, but can you feel the energy in the room?"

"Yes, it is very intense."

"Just give me a few minutes."

"Can you do this?" she asks. I wish she hadn't asked that question. It's one I never ask myself – I just assume that I can.

I am starting to realize that the energy in the room includes another, distinct energy in addition to those of Joe Cortez and my patient. This third energy is very strong and unusually big. I don't know if they have time, space, and dimension in the nonphysical world, but if the entity to whom this energy belongs were here in the physical world, he would be as big as a house. He is immensely powerful and staggeringly large. I say "he" because the energy seems masculine, but he is not human. He is something else, something different, and he is bigger in every way. He seems benevolent. And, thankfully, he is here to help. As his energy grows, I am asked to move away from the table. I am not asked with words, but the suggestion is placed into my mind.

"There's someone else here isn't there?" my patient asks. "Yes, he's really big."
"He's beautiful." She says.

As I move away from the table, I keep my energy connected, but I get as far away as possible. It's not that I am stopping working, it's just as if there isn't enough room in here for all of us. The energy of our visiting helper is so immense that it would be more comfortable in a football stadium or a canyon rather than in this small room. I find a place standing on a chair in the corner of the room. Even though I am deeply involved in this process, I can't help but notice how bizarre it is that I am standing on a chair in the corner of my own treatment room holding my hands out in the air like an idiot so I can rid this poor woman of the possessive spirit that has attached itself to her. It's totally crazy, yet here I am and I have to concentrate with every fiber of my being if I am going to see this through.

The immense energy-being has made it clear to me that he is here to help remove the attachment of Joe Cortez from my patient. However, the being is neither here for me nor for my patient, but for Joe Cortez himself. He and Joe Cortez have a relationship that is beyond my ability to understand. All I have to do is to stand here and hold the space so our big visitor can do his work. I don't know how much time has passed; maybe it's been about twenty or thirty minutes – it's getting hard to tell. My consciousness is sliding into another zone: I know I'm here, I can see everything and feel things normally, but I am more in another place.

I can tell there is some kind of negotiation going on between Joe Cortez and our big visitor. The big visitor has a fondness for Joe Cortez. He wants Joe Cortez to take his energy out of my patient's body and release his connection to her. Joe Cortez doesn't want to do this. I don't have complete access to what is going on. It is like watching an argument between two people in a foreign language. You can get the gist of it, but a lot of details are left out. I continue to stand on my chair in the corner with my arms held outward in order to hold the energetic space for this event to occur.

The big visitor is starting to do what I earlier tried and failed to do. He is lifting the energy of Joe Cortez out of my patient. I can feel it coming up. As his energy rises, I get a sense of what Joe Cortez is like, as a spirit. He is bursting with energy. He is playful. He is mischievous. Surprisingly, he is young. He is not an old spirit as I would have guessed. He is more like a child prodigy, enormously talented and gifted, but still a child. A six-year-old Mozart. He is bright and radiant...and then, in a moment, he is gone. He disappears out of my perception with his colossal guide about to follow behind him. I am freed from my position of holding the energy. The work is done.

The big Visitor is about to leave the room. He walks by me and casually says the words, "THANK YOU." The cursory utterance from this titan booms relentlessly throughout my being. The soundless sound is so loud that his words rack my entire body. I feel my every organ and bone vibrate as if I had been hit by a car going at a low speed and were knocked across the road, but not seriously hurt. My breath stops for a moment, and I have to compose myself. In a flash it comes to me that this being is not an advanced human spirit but an angel – or something similar to an angel – and that he has awesome power. I am glad to be on the right side of it.

"It's done isn't it?"

"Yeah, he just left."

"Oh my God. I haven't felt this light in years!" I wish I could say the same.

Commentary from Spirit

However intelligent, strong, or powerful you may be, there is always something greater. However kind and benevolent you may be, there are those kinder. Realize that you are like a child and there are those above you with strength and power who look down upon you with tender kindness.

Helping Plum to Die

Quote from Spirit

When death comes, open the door and fall into the loving arms of those who await you. Put away your fear, and delight in the awakening.

~Rayne

Sunday mornings I sleep late, but Bunnie gets up early. It is the day she calls her mother in England, who is in a home for the elderly in a part of the countryside called the Cotswolds. Her name is Anne Reeves, formerly Anne Lanchbury, born on January 2, 1920. She is 86 years old. Those who love her know her as Plum.

Every Sunday Bunnie spends as much time as possible on the phone with Plum. It is difficult for her to be so far away from her mother. Plum is in decline and Bunnie knows it. Plum's mind is getting farther and farther away from her body, the conversations are difficult and her memory is failing. Sometimes Plum doesn't know who Bunnie is, and sometimes Plum tells stories about things that have never happened. The calls always leave Bunnie in emotional turmoil. Between Sunday calls she always waits for that other call – the call that says she must catch the earliest flight to England.

Bunnie, who has no family other than an estranged sister, left England in her twenties and ever since has lived in Brazil and then America. She has a feeling that it's time to go to England for a visit, and, apologizing profusely (the British apologize a lot I'm finding out), asks me if I would go with her as a huge favor. I schedule a week off my clinic calendar, and we book a flight. British Airways has just started a nonstop flight from Phoenix

International to London-Heathrow, so we take advantage of an introductory offer. I'm excited – I've never been to England. Bunnie is uneasy. It has been a few years since she has visited Plum, and Bunnie is scared of how she might find her. I think it is helpful that I have never been to England. Introducing me to her country will help to take Bunnie's mind off her worry.

We book rooms at the Bibury Court Hotel, a seventeenth-century country manor not far from Plum's home and about two hours from London's Heathrow airport. The long international flight is blissfully uneventful. When we land I decide to splurge and rent a Jaguar. I just can't imagine spending my first time in England driving a Ford Escort. I like the Jag. It is British Racing Green, of course, with a cream leather interior, but there is the most peculiar thing about it. The steering wheel is on the wrong side! I forgot all about driving on the wrong side of the road. I have to shrug off jet lag and focus completely on keeping the car on the English side of the road. The first challenge is navigating the roundabouts, the little traffic circles that the English drive around to avoid having to put in stop signs and traffic signals. The circles make for a continuous flow of traffic through intersections, and they are kind of fun once you get the hang of them. We get on the motorway shortly after leaving the airport. Motorway is to England as freeway is to America, except nicer. The road is flat and smooth, and the drivers are courteous, use their turn signals, and stay out of the passing lane unless they are passing.

About twenty minutes down the motorway outside of London we pass Windsor Castle. The flag is flying on top, which means the queen is in residence. The Queen of England! I'm driving right by her house, in a Jag no less. I'm usually not a very good tourist, but here I am, getting all giddy about the queen being in residence as I drive by on the motorway. Suddenly, our Jaguar is passed by a red Ferrari Enzo, its one-million-dollar choir of angels trumpeting a twelve-cylinder harmony out the exhaust pipes. Now I really am giddy. Within an hour I see two Ferraris, three Aston Martins, a Maserati, a Lamborghini, and a Lotus Exige. I thought they only existed in glossy sports car magazines.

Beyond Windsor the countryside gets greener and greener. Beautiful rolling hills with cows and sheep and stands of forest are separated by pasture and crop lands. We follow the M4 Motorway to the A419 at Swindon. The "A" roads are more like highways – smaller than motorways and they don't have off-ramps, just regular junctions. At Cirencester we turn onto the B4425, the Burford Road, which will take us to the village of Bibury. "B" roads are two-lane country roads that sometimes squeeze themselves down to one lane without notice and then open out again into two. It's only fifteen minutes from Cirencester to Bibury.

The road to Bibury is lined with Cotswold dry stonewalls – miles and miles of longstanding walls built of rough-cut stones quarried locally and stacked by skilled hands. They have stood in place for centuries without the aid of cement or mortar. This type of wall exists only in the Cotswolds. We soon drive into Bibury, an old village of cottages and stone buildings. The village looks like it is out of a storybook. Tiny, slateroofed stone cottages perched precariously near the road watch our rented Jaguar roll by the same way they watched horse-drawn carriages roll by in their youth. As we drive through the village, the road narrows to one lane. At the narrowest point in the road there are no sidewalks – the stone walls of the old buildings thrust their ancient roots straight down through the asphalt at the edge the road. The old buildings, though originally placed far enough apart to allow passage of a horse and carriage, were not removed or relocated with the introduction of wider roads for automobiles. So when a two-lane road approaches one of these narrow passages, the white line in the middle simply disappears, leaving it up to the oncoming drivers to agree on who gets through the bottleneck first.

At the end of the village a small river runs through Bibury toward the trout farm. As we drive across the river over an arched stone bridge we see two white swans effortlessly floating downstream.

After the bridge we turn right, pass by the famous seventeenth-century Swan Hotel on the left, and then find our way through the narrow lanes to the Bibury Court Hotel.

The front lawn of the Bibury Court Hotel covers about four acres, and the road leading up to the house is gravel rather than blacktop, in keeping with the style of English country houses. The manor house is a large, rambling, three-story building made of hewn stone. Its grey walls have a centuries-old patina that make it look organic and alive rather than built. The Manor house was originally constructed in 1633 by Sir Thomas Sackville, a knight in waiting to King James. I can't help but be reminded of the Sackville-Baggins' from the Hobbit series. The whole of the Cotswolds looks like it might have sprang right from the chapter describing Middle Earth and the Shire. Around the year 1000AD the Saxons built the local church. And long before that the village of Bibury was first settled by the Romans.

The hotel's parking lot is filled with an eclectic collection of compact cars, sports cars, and Land Rovers. As we get out of our Jaguar, a man walks out of the hotel. He is in his late fifties and wears brown leather shoes, green corduroy trousers, a yellow vest, and a Harris Tweed sports coat. He gets into a dark green, convertible two-seater that says TVR, and nothing else, on the trunk lid. The motor growls to life like a wildcat, and he speeds off down the gravel road. Inside the hotel, the stone flooring is worn from the treading of hundreds of years of owners, guests, servants, and family members. A clean-cut young man in slacks and a tie shows us to our room. His family owns the hotel. There is no porter, no busboy, and no concierge. This is a country house, not a city hotel. My room has a carved, four-post bed with a hand-sewn quilt, and a wardrobe, a dresser, and a writing table – no television.

The window looks over the back garden and the trout stream, which gently winds its way through the countryside. The garden, in full bloom with mature plants and hedges, is reached by walking through a rose-covered archway that serves as an entrance to the verdant display of English landscaping. Over the back wall, is the church and its accompanying graveyard with ancient head stones leaning at odd angles.

At dinnertime Bunnie and I go down to an oak-paneled library where drinks are served, and our order is taken. A dozen or so people, separated into small groups, sit in plush leather couches and chairs. All the men have on jackets and slacks, including me. The women are all in dresses – casual, but nice, not showy or ostentatious. This is country casual, English style. The same young man who showed us in comes to take our dinner and drink orders. We sit on a big sofa with thick cushions and chat together as we sip cocktails and look out the paned windows at the sprawling four-acre lawn and beyond it where sheep graze on gently sloping, green hills. On the wall opposite us there is a large fireplace, which heats the room on cold English nights. The atmosphere is warm and cozy, and the guests are lively and friendly. I have yet to encounter the proverbial stuffy Englishman. In fact, everybody seems to be animated, engaging, and generally having a good time.

By the time we finish our drinks the young man comes in to tell us they are ready to seat us. A short walk down the stone corridor takes us to the dining room. The tables are dark mahogany and the chairs are covered in rich velvet. Our main course arrives as soon as we sit down, roast pheasant with mashed potatoes and fresh vegetables. The pheasant is tender and succulent with a wonderful, gamey flavor. It probably hadn't traveled more than three miles before it found our table. We take a walk around the garden after dinner, and then go off to our beds to sleep off the jet lag and get ready for tomorrow.

In the morning, we drive to visit Plum's home. Bunnie sits tensely in the passenger seat. I've heard so many stories about her idyllic upbringing. Plum was the perfect mother and wife. She was everybody's rock. Now everybody is gone except Bunnie, and Plum is very old. Plum has difficulty understanding what is happening to her. Bunnie prepares herself mentally and emotionally with nonstop chatting – it is her way. I am exactly the opposite, so it's hard for me to join in. I would be silent and introspective if I were in the same position. Bunnie is talkative and nervous. I do my best to help her feel comfortable, but I'm not the best at nervous chitchat and the conversation is stilted during our short trip.

Plum's home is a beautiful, old stone building in the Cotswold countryside. It looks like it must have been a manor house as well. But now it has everything necessary to help elderly and disabled people get around and feel comfortable. There are gentle slopes with handrails, elevators, and chair lifts. There is a large, beautiful, glass room on the side of the house. The British call it a conservatory. It's like a greenhouse, but for people instead of plants. There are several chairs and sofas with a gathering of elderly, grey-haired people enjoying the expansive view to the garden. We go in through the main entrance, where we are greeted by a smiling nurse dressed in a blue uniform with white edging and a small watch hanging from a pin attached to the fabric of her dress. She tells us that Plum is in the conservatory. Bunnie clutches my hands, digging her fingernails into my skin. She doesn't notice that she is about to draw blood. As soon as we walk into the room, Bunnie spots Plum sitting on a sofa. She is dressed in a long red and white plaid skirt, and matching jacket, and has had her hair done for the occasion. The home has a hairdresser who comes twice a month and for special occasions. Plum doesn't see us.

Bunnie lets go of my hand and walks straight to her. "Hello Plummy, it's me, Fats" – Bunnie's childhood nickname, which no longer applies to her figure.

"Hello, my dear, I'm so glad you are here."
"This is Michael, I told you about him on the phone."

"I'm very pleased to meet you," she says. She extends her hand in my general direction, but her eyes cannot find me. I grasp her hand to shake it. Her skin is soft and cool. I can tell she is from a time and place where extraordinarily good manners were considered mandatory.

"I'm very pleased to meet you as well. Bunnie has told me a lot about you."

"Oh, I don't think there is a lot to tell, is there dear?" she says to Bunnie.

I can see tears in Bunnie's eyes. She hugs her mother and tells her, "I love you so much, Plummy."

I decide to make myself absent for a few minutes so they can be together in private. After a long visit Bunnie and Plum come to find me in the lobby near the main entrance. They are hand in hand. Plum's barely five-foot frame looks thin and frail next to her daughter. Her steps are short and hesitant. Bunnie supports her from behind with her free hand.

"We've decided to go to lunch at Fromebridge Mill," Bunnie announces.

I bring the car around and load up Bunnie and Plum. We take Plum to lunch and try to keep the conversation upbeat, but I can see things are weighing heavily on Bunnie. Plum is completely exhausted after lunch. She can barely walk to the car even with me supporting most of her weight, but she is resolute and determined to make each step. We take her home and agree to meet again tomorrow.

"Thank you very much for taking me to lunch," Plum says in a feeble little voice as she extends her hand toward mine. I take her hand and kiss her on the cheek. "That was dainty," she says commenting on my tentative peck. So I offer a more robust kiss on the cheek to make up for it.

"Goodbye."

Bunnie and I get in the car to drive back to our hotel. Bunnie begins to cry as soon as we get into the car. She is an amazingly strong person, but seeing her mother, the rock of the family, in such a weakened state is too much for her. I wait quietly for a few minutes until she is ready to go.

The next day Plum is even weaker. Having us visit is too much for her. After a few minutes of talking, her mind begins to wander and she sleeps. Bunnie spends as much time as possible with her over the next few days, but as much as Plum wants to see her, she just doesn't have the stamina to keep up with even the smallest change to her daily routine. It is with sadness that we say goodbye to Plum and fly back to the US.

Two months later Bunnie gets the dreaded call from a nurse at Plum's home. Bunnie is asked to fly out as soon as possible. Bunnie says that she feels that she cannot ask me to put off my patients again, but she is dreading going alone. I assure her that it would be my privilege to help out in any way I can. There is no time for further discussion because we have to move fast. We are able to get the next flight out. Landing at London-Heathrow, we grab an econobox from Hertz and drive straight out to see Plum. When we arrive at the home, the same nurse greets us, but this time she is somber and solemn and her face wears no smile.

"I'm very glad you were able to get here so quickly. I'll take you to her."

We follow the nurse to Plum's bedroom. She is lying in her bed, the bones of her little body outlined by the bedding. Her eyes are open, but they show very little life. Her chest rises and falls with each labored breath. Bunnie kneels at her bedside and picks up her mother's thin hand. Plum turns her head toward Bunnie, and I catch a moment of recognition. I can see a beam of love transmitted from Plum to Bunnie. It is her last bit of energy, sent straight from a mother's heart to her daughter's. Then her consciousness disappears. She looks up again, but her eyes see nothing. Her breathing continues erratically and with great effort.

We stay at her side for hours, but she won't be returning to consciousness. We spend the night with her, but there is no change in the morning.

"You have to help her," Bunnie says to me.

"What do you mean? You know I can't help her. It's her time. There is nothing I can do."

"You have to help her pass. You have to make sure she is OK. I can't do it. She's my mother," she pleads.

I'm out of my depth. I have been with people while they are passing, but I never tried to intervene or to help in any way. But I can't refuse her request, so I put both feet on the floor, sit upright in my chair, and start to tune into Plum's energy. As soon as I get into the zone, I can sense that I am between two energies. One is Plum's, and the other is a group from the other side. They are here for her, but they are not connected to her yet. I can see immediately that I am to be used as an intermediary – a medium. I have to go between Plum's earthbound energy and this other group's higher, nonphysical energy and try to connect them. I close my eyes and place myself between them as a bridge. I am told to stop here. Don't do anything. Don't withdraw my energy and don't force my energy. They – the group on the other side – will direct things. I just do as I am told. Five minutes later, I am given the message to remove my energy. Then I am asked to offer my energy again a few minutes later. This continues for an hour, during which I am told when to engage or release my energy. I don't know exactly what is happening on the other side, but my directions are clear, so I follow them.

As I continue to work with Plum, I begin to feel very agitated and angry. I know this is completely inappropriate, but I can't help it, the feelings are so strong. I try to just sit still and relax, but that intensifies it. I tell myself to calm down and focus. Then, without warning, I jump two inches to the side and get shoved back in my seat. I can see a faint image of an old man standing in front of me with clenched fists. Suddenly, I am confused and worried. Did I do something wrong? Is someone angry with me, some spirit from the other side?

I tell Bunnie that I have to go to the bathroom, but really I need to get out of the room to get my head straight. In the hallway, I stand next to Plum's door and try to get a grip. I try to calm myself down. I'm here to help Bunnie and Plum, not to have my own breakdown. I tell myself to calm down and relax, but I feel my fists clenching in front of me like the old man in my vision. I'm talking outloud to myself. I see the nurse at the other end of the hall looking at me strangely. It's more than strange. Her eyebrows are raised and her eyes are opened wider than usual – she's scared. I immediately compose myself and smile at her. She smiles back and says something to another nurse, and then walks toward me.

"You alright?" she says in the local accent.

"Oh, yeah, thanks. I'm fine."

"You can see things, can't you? You were just standing here with your fists clenched just like the man who passed away used to do. Can you see him?"

Oh, now I get it. He has nothing to do with Plum. He found me because I am tuned into the spiritual energy. He is a wandering spirit who hasn't found his way out of the earthly grasp.

"Oh, is that what it is? I saw an old man with clenched fists."

"That's what he used to do – walk around with his fists clenched in front of him like he was angry, talking to himself. He passed away two weeks ago. There's another nurse here, she sees things. She saw him. Now you've seen him, too."

"Yes, I think I did."

"She said he was here. I'm going to tell her you saw him." She walks away purposefully.

In my minds eye I can see the old man nodding in agreement with the nurse, but he is still shaking his fists. He wants me to do something, but I am here for a different reason. I tell him I can't help him now and that he'll have to wait. Instantly, I feel normal again. The sense of anger and agitation has completely disappeared. Those weren't my own feelings after all. The anger and agitation didn't belong to me; they were his – transmitted to me while I was tuning into spiritual energy. I return to Plum's room, determined not to be distracted again.

Bunnie is still there holding Plum's hand, but Plum's consciousness is far away. I take my seat and begin to tune in. They are waiting for me. Instantly, I am told to hold my energy available for them. "Come on, Plum, you can do it," I hear a man's voice say, but I'm the only man in the room and I didn't say it. This voice is coming from somewhere else. He is excited and happy, not sad and mournful. "Come on, Plum, you can do it," he says again in an excited tone. He is encouraging her the way you would a child who is taking its first steps. It suddenly hits me. He is encouraging Plum to come over to the other side! I don't want to upset Bunnie any more than she already is, but I feel like I have to tell her about the voice.

"It's my father. He's here to help her. That's what he used to say – 'Come on Plum, you can do it!' He loves her. He's helping. He's there to meet her," she says, smiling through the tears in her eyes.

Another few minutes pass and I am told to take my energy away. I try to engage once more, but they don't need my help anymore. A few hours later, Plum's body stops breathing. I look for her energy; but it's not here; it has instantly ascended, and I can sense her presence very, very far away. She is in a place very high and very clear. On July 13, 2006, Anne Reeves ascended to a place too high for mere mortals to reach. We know from time to time she looks down upon us and gives her blessings.

Commentary from Spirit

Sooner or later the difficulties and challenges of this lifetime will be over. The body will cease and the true experience of being alive will begin. Free of the heavy weight of earthly existence, the spirit can ascend to its proper place in the next world. It will be a meeting of friends and loved ones, some known in this lifetime, others known previously.
Sense of purpose will be understood and loving connections will be reinstated.

Making Love to Angels

Quote from Spirit

"Do not attach, but instead, let go. Let go of your desire."
~I Lin

The Cotswolds have left an impression on me – the nice people, the pubs, the storybook-like rolling green hills with cows and sheep happily leading their pastoral lives. Maybe it's just the stark contrast with the desert. Maybe it's the basic agreeable, communal nature of the Cotswold dwellers versus the rugged, individualist heritage of the desert folks. The Cotswold hobbits seemed gentler and more civilized than the desert men and women. Bunnie admits that since her mom passed away she has been feeling drawn back to England where she grew up. I am finding that my own romance with the desert has passed. We decide to sell the big house and follow new paths.

The big house is beautiful, grand, and elegant. It's a wonderful showpiece and great place to have my clinic, but eight-thousand square-foot, open-floor-plan homes are not everyone's first choice for an abode. Its worst feature is the kitchen, the most important selling point after location. The heating and cooling is out of date, and the layout is extremely strange, with a fifteen-by-sixty-foot-long hallway and two thousand square feet of living room and family room area. When we first inquired about the house, the real estate agent didn't even want to show it to us. It had been two years on the market, and she thought it was a lost cause. And now, I've got to sell it.

Living in a house that is on the market is a life of continuing worry and stress. At any time an agent could call wanting to show the house – and they always want to show it now! The clients are in the car, they just drove by, and they want to see the inside. They can wait maybe an hour while they look at another house, but then they are flying back to wherever they came from. So we run, we vacuum, we clean. They come. They look. They leave. All with patients coming and going. This goes on week after week, month after month. The stress builds and we never seem to have any relief.

Tonight, I go to bed with a tension in my heart. It's almost a pain. My God, is this what happens to people before they have a heart attack? Am I one of these stressed-out guys who is so consumed with business, money, and life that he gives himself a heart attack worrying about it? No. I'm nowhere near a heart attack, but still, I am having direct physical symptoms of stress. This has to stop.

As I lay my head down on the pillow, I can tell sleep is not going to come easily. I close my eyes and try to relax. I'm too uptight about selling the house to do my usual three lines qigong meditation. I just lie here on my side and try to calm my mind. Suddenly, I feel a sensation like someone is putting a blanket on my shoulders from behind, and my entire visual field behind my closed eyelids starts changing to a light tan color. It's as if a can of tan paint had been dumped on the back of my eyelids and the paint is oozing down the inside turning the whole field to the new color. The feeling of the blanket clinging to my body from shoulders to feet seems to coincide with the oozing of the tan paint down the back of my eyelids. My whole body relaxes as the paint covers my visual field. I hear a calm and confident male voice in my head say with amazing clarity: "TRUST." That's it. No more, just "trust." Then the tan color dissipates, as does the feeling of being wrapped in a blanket, but the relaxation stays. I go to sleep and wake up the next morning refreshed, confident, and ready for another day in clinic.

A tall, thin, attractive blond woman in her forties sits in my treatment room. She is wearing a long, flowing, mauve dress made of layers of diaphanous material. She has large silver rings with bright stones on most of her fingers, a big turquoise and silver necklace, and earrings that hang down onto her neck. She is sitting cross-legged with one foot gently bobbing up and down. She smiles and looks at me with half-closed, sultry eyes as I enter the room. This is going to be interesting.

"Hi, I'm Michael," my usual.

"Hello," she breathes.

"What can I do for you?"

"I want to be in perfect balance and radiate love, health, and beauty."

OK, it beats low back pain, menstrual cramps, and bloating. "Oh, that should be achievable."

"Anything else?" I chirp back to her.

"No," she smiles.

I motion for her to get onto the table. She moves slowly and gracefully as she mounts the treatment table and rolls onto her back. She closes her eyes and takes a long, slow, deep breath in, then exhales with a barely audible moan as her arms drop to her sides. She is ready.

I extend my arms with palms facing down so that my hands are about a foot over her body and wait. She takes another long, slow breath as I begin to work. This time she exhales a distinctly audible moan. As I explore her energy field I come into contact with an energy blockage, and she responds with a visible shiver through her body.

"Can you feel him?" she asks.

"I can feel something." It definitely feels like there is male energy attached to her. I start to work to define it, so I can help her remove this attachment.

"He makes love to me"

"Who is that?" I ask, trying to sound clinical and objective.

"The Archangel Michael. I can feel him in me when you touch his energy."

The Archangel Michael makes love to you? I've seen enough strange and interesting things that even now I will suspend disbelief and wait to see what happens.

"Does this happen often?"

"He comes to me almost every night," she smiles.

I continue to focus on the energy blockage that I have found. I continue to define it. It is male and it is very sexual, but it is no angel. The energy is dark, and it is angry and jealous at my presence in what it considers to be its domain, but I can tell he doesn't have the kind of power that is dangerous to me. I continue to corral his energy, so I can remove it from this patient.

"Have you ever considered that this energy could be from someone else?" I ask.

"What do you mean?" she asks flatly with a cold voice.

"I mean how do you know it is who it says it is?"

She opens her eyes and looks penetratingly at me. "I know exactly who it is. If you can't handle it, then you should let me know," she barks in an angry tone.

"So, you don't want me to do anything with this energy that's inside you?"

"We are together. I want to radiate the beauty that I feel within," she purrs and smiles.

"Just to be clear, you want me to leave his energy here and work around it. Is that right?"

"Oh, yes. Definitely don't touch his energy if you are planning on moving it. I want him right where he is." Can't be clearer than that.

There is nothing I can do for her. I continue to do a fluff and buff on her energy systems and then say goodbye.

I know that it is possible to have interactions with nonphysical entities. I have had them. I think we can even communicate with angels – my session with Joe Cortez proved that to me. Joe's guide was, I believe, an angel or some other superior being that does not exist in our terrestrial lexicon. When that being merely said a casual thank-you to me, I almost had my organs scattered from the sheer force of energy. If I'd had an intense direct interaction with him, I probably wouldn't be here in one piece today. In contrast to the immensity of the angel's energy is this angry little lump of dark energy that has enthralled my love-struck patient. Like an abusive spouse, he is very jealous and controlling. It is hard to imagine, even with the widest latitude, that he is an angel. Yet she is convinced that this poor spirit is the Archangel Michael.

I ask Bunnie if her spiritist group had ever run into this kind of thing.

"It's fascination," she says.

"What's fascination?" I ask.

"That's what we call it in Portuguese. In Brazil, we see this often," Bunnie explains, "especially with people who, though sensitive to spirits, are not truly skilled in how to interact with spirits and how to interpret their interactions. This woman is fascinated by her interaction with this entity, who is controlling her by proxy. He told her that he is the Archangel Michael, and her ego let her believe him. Now, he draws her energy from her during their love making."

"He is an incubus!" I exclaim. That makes perfect sense. "What is an incubus?"

"It is a nonphysical being who takes women's energy through sex. The male version of a succubus."

"We simply call it fascination. It is a minor form of possession. He will not let her go. She is fascinated by their relationship. It is difficult, because there is nothing you can do without her agreement, and she will not agree as long as she remains fascinated."

The relationship serves both her ego and his need to dominate. It's a form of possession. Not the head-spinning-around and pea-soup-flying-everywhere kind of possession, but a minor form where both parties are in agreement, even though one is deluded. Maybe the weirdest thing is that she was the second patient that I have had in the last month who believes she makes love to the Archangel Michael. I wonder if it is the same entity? He must get around.

Two weeks later a real estate agent calls to say she has a client looking for a house just like ours, and she wants to show it this afternoon. Good thing it's Sunday and we don't have clinic. Same drill – run, vacuum, clean. They come, they look, they leave, but they don't drive away. They linger by the gate for half an hour. This is a good sign! The next day an offer is presented. In the following days, I get along very well with the buyer – we are able to agree on a price, and he is kind enough to allow us enough time to wind up the clinic.

I am feeling guilty about leaving my patients. Thankfully, none of them at this time except one, Brad, are in a terrible state of health that requires my regular attention. A few may be emotionally dependent on me; this will be a good way to wean them. Amazingly, Brad, who needs my work the most, is the patient who is happiest for me in my new adventure. I will miss all of them.

Commentary from Spirit

When you love, remember there is only one love. When you desire, remember there is only one desire. Attune yourself to the Great Love and make it your one desire.

The Saint with the Golden Cross

Quote from Spirit

There is power greater than you know. You will connect to it in many forms when you are ready.
~William

Drawn back to the Casa de Dom Ignacio, I decide to make another visit to Brazil before leaving Arizona. Once again, I travel to Abadiania and find a room at one of the many pousadas springing up along the main road that leads to the Casa. This time it's all business for me: I'm not here as a tourist; I'm here to get something done. I don't know exactly what it is, but I do know that I'm about to make some kind of shift deep inside. I have to stay focused. The walk to the Casa is shorter this time and my room is luxurious by comparison. It's even got an air conditioner.

I have a better understanding of how things work at the Casa and what to expect. During the healing sessions the consciousness of the man, John of God, leaves his body giving control of it over to powerful spiritual entities. He is wholly unaware of the amazing healing work that is done through his body in his absence. Only at the end of the morning or afternoon sessions does John of God's own consciousness return to his body. Over a hundred meditators all dressed in white, sit in service, giving their energy to help with the work. Some of the more experienced meditators have special duties such as helping to protect the area from the unwanted intrusion of lower spiritual entities. When the veil is pierced and the doorway to spiritual energies is open, it is critical that unfriendly spirits don't wander in and disrupt the healing sessions.

A horrible shrieking of a wild animal cuts the air, as I enter the main hall of the Casa. Maybe it's a wild pig, as the Casa is in a rural area at the edge of town. Perhaps it wandered in during the night and didn't waken until all the people showed up. It probably can't find it's way out because of all the people, and it's panicking. The shrieking is loud and frightening – maybe it's injured. People are crowding around – the animal must be freaking out. They should get out of the way and let it escape. The shrieks begin to change into an almost human sound. It must be getting tired. A long wailing noise starts and continues for a few minutes; then a frenzied shrieking starts again with loud panting in between squeals and howls. It is sounding more human as it goes on. All at once, I realize that this is not an animal: it is a person, but not the voice of a person. I wedge myself into the crowd to get a better look.

Lying on the floor of the main hall is a young woman in her twenties or early thirties. She is thin with short black hair. Her eyes are clamped shut, and she is writhing around in a fetal position right in front of the door that leads into John of God's chamber. As I see her she starts wailing again, but this time she is speaking in words. "I can't go in there. He'll kill us. He'll kill us! He'll kill me if I go in there." There are several Casa attendants standing around her. Most of them are praying. Two of them are sprinkling holy water on her head and body. The girl's parents are standing with her. After a few dowsings with holy water, the attendants are able to get the young woman to her feet. Her parents, one on each side, steady her as the door opens. They take her in to be attended by the powerful spiritual being that is now incorporated into the body of John of God. I don't see her again.

A speaker on the stage in the main hall begins reciting the Lord's Prayer over the microphone, and then follows with the Ave Maria. Most of the crowd joins in the recitation. I don't know the words by memory, so I mumble along with the crowd. With the recitation

144

of the prayers the whole ambience changes to a calm and mellow vibe. I can hear two Brazilian women behind me speaking in Portuguese, "A menina estava possuida por um espirito maligno." The girl was possessed by an evil spirit. "Devemos rezar por ela." We must pray for her.

As a returning person who has passed before John of God in prior visits, I'm not allowed into the first-timer line this morning. I have to come back in an hour or so to stand in the returning-line. So I wander out to the observation deck where I sat last time I was here. There are many people sitting on the deck, but the view is still peaceful. I sit on a bench and close my eyes. Immediately, I feel subtle sensations of multiple energies around and throughout my body, as if I am being checked over by some invisible triage team, as happened once before during my first visit to the Casa. Each of my chakras gets a quick look, starting from the base up to the crown. As they inspect me, a tight knotted feeling tells me which of my chakras need the most help – base, heart, and throat. It takes only about a minute before the unseen visitors finish their assessment and move on. It is now very clear to me that all the spiritual work I have been doing in the clinic has made me much more sensitive than I was the first time I came here.

I leave the observation deck and wander around the compound, trying to stay away from both visitors and attendants. I really need to stay focused because I feel that a change is coming that will restructure my energy. I don't know how I know, but I know. I don't want to get caught up in any distractions, so I keep to myself. After forty-five minutes I head back to the main hall and get into the returning visitor line and wait. I feel several different conscious entities as they move invisibly by me. I don't know exactly what they are doing, possibly a sort of triage like the one I experienced out at the observation deck a few minutes ago. Whatever it is, it must be part of the invisible service at the Casa de Dom Ignacio.

Another hour and the line begins to file into John of God's chamber.

As soon as I walk in I start to feel energy buzzing just under my skin. John of God is sitting in his chair, briefly talking to each person who passes him. As I get closer, my body starts to tremble and tears begin to flow out of my eyes. The closer I get, the more the trembling intensifies. When I find myself standing in front of John of God, he looks at me with kind eyes and asks, "What is your work?" I reply that I'm an acupuncturist and I do spiritual work. He tells me to take off my watch and to sit and wait. One of his assistants pulls me out of line and directs me to an empty chair about ten feet away from John of God. I can barely make it to the chair because I'm shaking so much. I feel like my legs are going to buckle. I put my watch in my pocket and sit down on the chair as my body continues to shake violently.

My eyes are clamped shut, tears streaming out of them. I can feel my left hand, the one that had the watch on, rising up off my lap to roughly head height, palm facing outward. I'm not initiating the action. It's happening of its own volition. About fifteen feet above me and to the right I can feel a presence of some powerful being. It's huge. It exudes compassion. Then, in my mind's eye, images of all of the patients I have treated over the years shuffle in front of me in rapid succession and then disappear. The presence, which seems to be hovering above me, directs my attention to a mental image of an individual who is physically a great distance away. I can only describe the image as an essence of the actual person. Thoughts come pouring into my head so fast that I feel like I'm going to overflow. It's as if I were in a teaching hospital and the chief surgeon is presenting a real patient for instructional purposes. The presence is teaching me.

For at least twenty minutes I sit shaking and weeping, my left hand in the air with palm facing outward. I am taken through a series of treatment protocols, each of them seeming to have a different effect

146

on the essence seen in the distance. I am being shown how to identify certain kinds of blockages and different ways of dealing with them.

I begin to use one of the methods the spiritual being has shown me on the distant patient. I am removing layers of dark energy. I can tell after removing several of these layers that my own energy is becoming depleted and that the distant patient's layers are so many and so deep that I am not strong enough to take them all off. Next, I am shown what appears to be an advanced protocol, a method of completely transforming the essence of the individual in question. The being guides my hand and my energy as we work on the patient together. I feel like I did as a child when I sat on my fathers lap and steered the car, his hands over mine making sure the car stayed on the road.

I realize the patient's darkness is so deep and has so many layers that it cannot be uncovered one layer at a time. The powerful being, whom I can now see clearly, is dressed in a plain brown robe and carries a large gold cross in his hand. He is showing me how to get straight to the true essence of the individual without uncovering each layer one at a time. My body is shaking violently, and it is difficult to maintain my mental composure, but I have to stay with the process. This may be my only chance to learn from this extraordinarily powerful entity, this saint in a brown robe. I give everything I have to this moment. My body is still trembling with my hand raised in the air, and tears are streaming down my face as I continue to sit in the chair near John of God. The reality of the man in the brown robe, the essence of the poor soul in the distance, and the work that I am doing now are more real to me than my physical body and the physical environment. I am totally and completely present in this nonphysical reality, a spiritual dimension more real than the physical world. Guiding my hand – actually guiding my energy – the robed saint stretches our energy out into space to the tortured and desperate figure. I know that I, by myself, do not have the strength to relieve his dark burdens. The man in the robe understands this. He is showing me another way.

He guides me to go straight to the pure essence of the patient. As I do this, I falter for a moment, feeling afraid and inadequate. I don't think I can do it. I don't have the strength or the ability. Suddenly, the saint summons an enormous amount of energy. Like a tidal wave, he lifts me up emotionally and spiritually, and he also lifts the pure essence of the patient at the same time. The saint then delivers a crushing blow to both the patient and myself as his hand holding the golden cross comes crashing downward upon us. Golden light flashes in all directions, emanating from where the cross lands its blow. I feel a huge expansion of my own energy as I watch the patient's essence get seared and branded with the energy from the golden cross wielded by the saint. My experience is exactly the opposite of passing out; rather, it's as if I am being super-awakened beyond normal senses. Together, with the saint in the brown robe, and with my hand still being guided by his, we pull the patient's pure essence free from the heavy layers of darkness. We hold him bare and pure in front of us and above his discarded burdens of heavy, dark energy. At that moment the high being transmits the thought that the patient's path has been cleared. If the patient decides to raise himself from his low position and get on with his life, then that possibility will be available to him – but the choice remains his own. Either way, he will no longer be rendered helpless by his burdens.

With the reverberations of the mighty crash subsiding, the high spirit lets me go. I am released. The patient is no longer part of my awareness. My hand drops to my lap, and I begin to feel like I am in my body instead of out in another realm of reality. As if answering a question that I had not yet formed, the thought is transmitted into my mind that I will be able to help people from a distance. My body stops shaking, and I am completely and utterly exhausted. I stay in my seat until the morning session is over, and then I file out with the meditators and head back to my room.

I hit the bed and sleep for 12 hours, only getting up for the bathroom and to take a few sips of water. I wake groggy and lethargic the next morning. The window is open in my room, and I can hear people eating in the outdoor dining area. I think about getting up, but I don't want to see anyone right now. I'm feeling too raw, too vulnerable. I didn't know the reason from coming to the Casa when I booked the trip, but now the purpose has been made clear and I am absolutely confident it has been fulfilled.

Even though I am not Catholic, I am encouraged to attend mass that evening.

(Santa Theresa and the Disco Priest)

The priest and his entourage roll in around 9PM for an 8 O'clock mass. He is short and slightly round with a kind face, carrying a large heavy looking new black suitcase. His assistants, are dressed to party. The girl, late teens or early twenties, in a blue a chiffon dress that fits snuggly and ends well above her matching blue pumps. The boy, about the same age, sports skin tight designer bluejeans with sequins down both sides, a western style dress shirt pearl snap-buttons and pointy-toed cowboy boots and carrying a huge plastic and chrome boom box. Both of them wear pious expressions.

We sit quietly in the front row of folding steel office chair makeshift pews. When I can finally tear my gaze away from the man of God and his acolytes, I bend my head in meditation or is it prayer? Anyway, I quiet my mind and sit. People from the Casa sit next to me with there bodies in the same position.

The shiny suit case thumps down on the tile floor a few feet in front of me. Buckles snap open. Gleaming, bright, untouched, brand spanking new goblets, garments, vials, and incense all neatly folded and packed, shine forth. The Acme All in One Sacrament

Kit for Beginners and Pros alike. The young priest reverentially unfolds the white garment and slips it over his head, and over his pressed bluejeans. His assistants set up the boom box.

I close my eyes again. A surge of energy washes through my body. I immediately have the sense of a beautiful feminine presence above me. I lean over to tell the person next to me what I feel, but she has her eyes close tightly and her body is tense. Entranced. I look up to try to see the energy that I feel from above and have to blink several times. A bust of a woman in a nuns habit with a crucifix around her neck materializes up in the rafters of the building. It's like a silhouette or a transparency or a hologram. When I see her, feelings of love, compassion, and a kind of religious ecstasy take over my senses. My body starts to sweat and my cheeks flush.

Then they hit it. Bumpa chinka, bumpa chinka. The boom box kicks in at full volume as the priest takes the stage. His acolytes are posted in front at either side of the podium. Boy nearest the boom box. Bumpa chinka, bumpa chinka. Brazilian pop. Let us pray.

I tear my eyes from this fantastic spectacle only to fix them on another one. She is still there, the nun. Bumpa chinka, bumpa chinka. Tears begin to well up in my eyes. Out of her forehead shoots the shape of a cross, well more like a T, a cross with the top missing. It's like a spotlight beaming straight down toward us, onto the forehead of the woman next to me. It hits her and her body goes rigid and she shakes violently like a thousand volts just plugged into her. I look at the person next to her, but he is looking up at the nun and doesn't notice womans's convulsions.

"Why is everybody so unhappy when they pray? You shouldn't have a face like you just got a speeding ticket. You should look like your team just won the World Cup! Who is your favorite team? GOD! Celebrate!" The priest waves his hands in the air. His acolytes smile. Hit it. The priest points a John Travolta disco finger at the boy. A new track is selected. Same as the old track. Bumpa chinka, bumpa chinka.

Another disco finger and silence. The woman next to me is breathing erratically and sweating. I don't see the nun anymore. "Receive Jesus Christ into your hearts." A moment of silence. Dee do dee dee do dee dee. The priest looks at the young man who shrugs. He looks at the girl who checks her purse for her cell phone. The boy reaches for his, Dee do dee dee do dee dee. They both furiously stab buttons on their tiny phones trying to shut off the annoying racket. Finally the priest beams a broad smile and hikes up his white garment, reaches into the back pocket of his bluejeans an whips out a chrome cased cell phone, silences the tinny caterwauling then quickly shoves it back into his pocket and regains his form. Disco finger. Bumpa chinka, bumpa chinka.

Everyone is invited, Catholics and non-Catholics alike, to partake in sacrament. There is a genuine kindness and love emanating from the young priest. He is doing God's work. His flock are receiving the blood and the body of Christ. The foreigners have been inducted as family. Peace and love fill the hearts of all those in attendance.

Commentary from Spirit

There are many high beings who have once lived here on Earth. Some of them are known in various religions as saints and prophets, and by other names. Most are not known at all.

To interact with them from afar, through their chain of spiritual energy is very common, to interact with them in their direct presence can be an intense and amazing experience.

In your spiritual growth and maturation, whether in this lifetime or in another you will meet and interact with great beings. Some of them greater than you can imagine.

Space Needles

Quote from Spirit

"What is far away is close. What is near is illusion."
~I Lin

A dentist's drill, a red hot poker, a paper cut. We all have our own ideas of pain, mild or severe. To most of us simply banging our knee or our funny bone really hurts, but the pain can still be considered mild, whereas labor pain or the pain of breaking a major bone can be considered severe. There is, however, a whole other realm of physical pain, the kind of intense and extreme pain that can only be understood by those who suffer it. The kind of pain that makes a grown man drop to his knees and scream a silent scream when he would have screamed aloud, but his whole body is frozen rigid by a terrible sensation beyond description. Or the kind of fiery, piercing pain you might imagine in a nightmarish horror film where someone strapped to a dentist's chair writhes in agony as the shock of the dentist's drill electrifies the raw nerve of her tooth. This is a whole other world of pain: this is trigeminal neuralgia.

Brad first came to me five years ago. He is a tall, strong man who used to run a trucking company. He has been diagnosed with multiple sclerosis, a debilitating disease that covers the motor nerves in a white plaque that eventually renders them useless. It is a slowly progressing condition in which the victim loses muscle coordination, loses the ability to walk, and often dies with related complications after decades of suffering. Although most people with MS can live a productive life and have many good years after onset, it's not something you would wish on your worst enemy. It's bad enough for anyone to have to deal with MS, but it's nothing compared with the chronic and severe pain of trigeminal neuralgia. At least that's Brad's opinion – and he's got both.

Brad came to me as a referral from a psychic consultant whom I've never met. That seemed very strange to me at the time. Now, however, it seems perfectly reasonable, a testimony to how much my views have changed in the past few years on certain ideas that I had long considered to be fuzzy thinking.

When Brad first came to see me I had just moved from Grant Road to the house with the ghost that Bunnie exorcised. When he arrived, he leaned heavily on a walker and slowly made his way into my treatment room. He told me about his MS and about the pain associated with his trigeminal neuralgia. He explained that he had seen many doctors, neurologists, acupuncturists, and energy workers. But none of them improved his condition, and some of them had made it worse. Brad was happy to see me on the referral of his psychic consultant under one condition—that I would not actually touch him. This was the first time I had had this particular request from a patient. He was scared that if I touched him I might make the trigeminal pain worse. It reminded me of stories my Chinese medicine teachers used to tell in acupuncture school about Imperial Court physicians who were not allowed to touch the emperor's concubines. Instead, a concubine patient would tie a string around her wrist that was threaded through a small opening in a curtain separating the concubine from the physician. The physician would

touch the string to assess the patient's pulse and make a diagnosis. Not touching Brad meant that I would not be able to do acupuncture or any type of hands-on work, leaving me only with qigong, a no- touch type of energy work. Up until this point, I had only used qigong in association with other clinical modalities such as acupuncture. I explained to Brad that it wouldn't be a problem, because I would use this therapy to adjust his energy. He hesitated for moment and then explained that in the past he had also received energy work, which made the pain a lot worse. This left me in a bit of a bind, but after some negotiation he agreed to allow me to use the qigong therapy. When I first came into contact with his energy he began to feel the pain getting worse. I could tell that the blockage was about to release, so I assured him that if he stuck with it for a few more minutes it would subside. We managed to get a reasonable amount of improvement and he continued to work with me to manage his pain. He stayed in treatment with me for the following five years. With some ups and downs, I was able to help change the intolerable to tolerable, but just barely.

Brad was one of the few patients I was really worried about at the time I closed my clinic in Tucson. Some patients were upset or angry at me for leaving, but Brad never had anything to say other than he wished me well. I knew he was scared. Nobody else had been able to help him much with his pain, and my leaving meant he would be without his safety net.

Eight months after leaving Tucson, I receive an email that Brad is suffering terribly with his trigeminal neuralgia.

"Hi, Marilyn, it's Michael Roland. I got your email."

"Hi Michael. Brad's having a really rough time. He's been in pain for a long time now."

"Is he still seeing the acupuncturist I referred?"

"He's not really able to talk and he can't eat or drink because of the pain. We've got him taking as much morphine as we can. The doctors have him on intravenous nutrition and hydration. It's been going on for about three months now. You're not coming back anytime soon are you?" she joked.

"Why didn't you call me?"

"You're in Thailand!" She had a point there. I started to think about the thought message that I received from the brown-robed saint in Brazil. He said I would be able to do my work from a distance. Does that go for acupuncture?

"Well, I won't be coming out anytime soon, but if Brad is willing, we can try a little experiment."

"Michael, I think he is willing to try anything."

"Well, this might sound weird, but you've known me long enough now to know weird is normal. I want to try doing some distant acupuncture on him."

"We'll try anything, Michael."

"OK, I'll call you on Skype in a half an hour and we'll start." "I'll make sure Brad is in front of the computer."

From a course on ear acupuncture I took a few years earlier, I recalled the instructor's story about Paul Nogier, a famous French acupuncturist considered the father of ear acupuncture. Although Nogier's early work in ear acupuncture was well respected, he was always experimenting to further develop his art. Over the years he deepened his understanding of acupuncture, though many thought that he had gone off the deep end. Students who attended his workshops to see an ear acupuncture demonstration might find Dr. Nogier holding needles several inches to several feet away from his subjects, needling their auras instead of their ears. At this point he would be trotted off the stage, and the workshop would get back to legitimate acupuncture. Our instructor conveyed this story with some sense of sadness and dismay. My immediate impression, however, was that Nogier's work in acupuncture had simply evolved to another level – it represented a deeper understanding of the nature of energy medicine.

While I was in that other space – the other reality – under the spiritual guidance of the saint in the brown robe, it was obvious that space is an illusion. In the moment, I understood it perfectly. If space is an illusion, then distance should have no effect. Maybe this was the case both with Nogier, who could do acupuncture from three feet away, and with the ancient Chinese physicians who could diagnose patients by touching a string connected to their patients' wrists. If acupuncture can be done at a distance, can it be done from any distance? Is space relevant for the physical body, but not for the life energy associated with it? Does qi exist in space or irrespective of it?

It's interesting to theorize, but Brad is not a theory – he's a real person with terrible pain. He has used up all his options and I must try to help him. I retrieve a set of needles that I never travel without then return to my computer. How am I going to do this? Maybe if I had a little voodoo doll, I could needle it in acupuncture points? But I don't have one. The ringing of an old-fashioned phone comes from my computer, signaling that they have Brad ready for his experimental treatment. I answer the Skype request and see a video image of Brad on my computer monitor. He is in bed with no shirt on – it's hot in Arizona. He looks emaciated and off-color. I have always liked Brad. I'm glad to be in contact again, even under these difficult circumstances. When Brad's pain is too much for him to talk, he keeps a chalkboard nearby. The computer image of Brad waves hello to me, and then it lifts up a small chalkboard that just has "PAIN BAD" scrawled onto it.

I speak into the microphone. "Yeah, I've heard, Brad. Sounds pretty rough. I want you to know that I have no idea if this is going to work, but if you are willing, we're going to give it a try." He scribbles on his chalkboard: "OK"

I still haven't figured out how I'm going to do it yet, so I think fast. I ask Brad to point to where the pain is, the same way I used to do when he came into my clinic as a patient. He points to his lower jaw line on the right side along the line of the lower branch of the trigeminal nerve. I take a moment to palpate the acupuncture points on my own body that I would normally associate with this kind of pain. I find the ones I like, then insert the acupuncture needles into my own skin. I tell Brad to just relax and wait.

After a few minutes I ask how the pain is. He scribbles "Better."

"OK, let's keep working at it." It could be psychosomatic; maybe he just wants it to be better, so he feels like it is working. We need to keep testing it. After another twenty minutes I ask again.

"How's the pain?"
"Better" his chalkboard replies.
"How much better? Ten percent, twenty percent, ninety percent?"
"20"
"OK, let's keep at it."

After an hour we have a solid twenty percent improvement. So we keep working an hour a day for the next three days. Brad's pain reduces steadily. With some string and a few banana leaves from the local Thai restaurant's outdoor kitchen, I fashion a crude equivalence of a human figure. Instead of needling myself, I start to needle the doll. To my surprise, I can feel the energy more clearly through the doll than I could through my own body. Maybe it's because I get less interference from my own body's energy this way. For whatever reason, it works. I'm glad for Brad, and I'm glad for myself – I've never much liked getting stuck with needles.

After five sessions, we scale back to three times a week. Brad is able to talk, eat, and drink again within two weeks. Success! I would rather be able to cure him completely, but fifteen years in the clinic has made me realize that cures don't come along nearly as often as you hope, but if you try hard, most of the time you can make a difference.

I treat a few other people and find that I am able to get results with them as well. The fact that it works leaves me with more questions than answers. Is it placebo? Is it fantasy? Does Brad only imagine his pain is lessening or is it exactly what it appears to be: an energetic connection that disregards space, or perhaps the illusion of space, and directly affects Brad's energetic system to bring about much needed comfort and relief? In time, science will find answers and explanations to the question of how distance-healing works just as it discovered the shape of the earth, continental drift, and subatomic forces. For now, I'm just happy that I can help in this small way.

Commentary from Spirit

We live an illusion, but it is the nearest we can come to reality. Space and time are constructs of the relative reality that we find ourselves living within. The closer we get to the ultimate truth, the thinner the more transparent the illusion becomes. So, engage fully in the relative reality in which you find yourself, but keep your senses open to a higher truth.

Time Tunnels

Quote from Spirit

When you hurt others, you hurt yourself. It is your pain that binds you to the pain of others. Unravel your bindings and dance in Glorious Light!

~Rayne

All forms of medicine have a set of tools and techniques that have an effect on the patient. In surgery, scalpels and sutures are used to cause change in the physical body that will lead to better health. An acupuncturist uses needles to manipulate qi in a way that will lead to better health. Obviously, the surgeon must be physically present to use her scalpel on the patient's body. I always assumed that the acupuncturist must also be present to use his needles on the patient's acupuncture points. However, in Brad's treatment the needles were placed in a surrogate model in Thailand yet the changes were effected within Brad's body in America. Their power to manipulate qi was not obstructed by distance. The success with Brad's treatment demonstrated to me that energy work does not depend on proximity.

During the last two years of my practice in Tucson, I spent at least half of my treatment hours doing some form of qigong-energy or spiritual work. Most of that work was done at distances varying from several inches up to several feet without ever physically touching my patients. I always assumed that it was important for my patients to be with me in the room, in close physical proximity. But was it? Would the energy work have been any different or less effective from a distance?

As I am considering these questions, an email shows up from Jodie, one of my Tucson patients. She is expressing distress about some issues that came up during one of our qigong sessions back in Tucson. I reply to her that we can investigate the issues from a distance if she is interested. She agrees, and we set an appointment for an internet telephone call between Thailand and Tucson.

At the appointed hour, 10 o'clock at night in Thailand, 8 AM in Tucson, I contact Jodie. After we exchange greetings I tell her I am going to tune into her energy. I know what her energy will feel like because I have worked with her before. Within seconds I connect, and it's definitely her energy. I can tell because of the familiar emotional sensations specific to her energy pattern. In effect, we now have two long-distance calls going at the same time between Thailand and Tucson: one by means of internet voice technology and the other by means of human qi technology. I'm really excited. I didn't know if this was going to work, but her energy patterns are as clear to me from this enormous distance as they were when we shared the space of the same treatment room in Tucson. What's strange is that her energy is actually clearer and easier to read from this distance. Could it be because there is no interference from the proximity of her body and the energy that it produces? Whatever the reason, it is obvious to me that we are in energetic contact, and it is clearer than ever before.

It is as if we are in the same room. So I begin to work in the way that I always have. After the initial contact with her energy, I begin to sink into Jodie's energetic system. This sinking-in step takes some moments during which there isn't much information available. It's a process of gently entering deeply into her energy system without causing upset.

Next, I begin to locate and identify energy blockages – and she has several. The big ugly one, right up front, is anger. She carries this anger with her all the time. Whenever there is provocation, real or imagined, she will trot it out with all its wrath. Those around her will suffer the brunt of her hidden anger and feel it as disproportionate to the insult, but she will feel it is justified because her anger tells her so. This is her biggest blockage and I want to deal with it first, but I can't because there are other energy blockages competing for my attention. Each person's energy is self-organizing. It often has levels or hierarchies and a particular order in which problems should be processed. I always follow the natural progression offered by the client's energy; I never dictate it.

The other energy blockages that I must first attend to are the usual suspects. An ex-boyfriend is first. But it's not his energy that wants the attention – it's hers. An aspect of Jodie's energy is telling me it needs help. It's like a dog walking up to you on three legs, holding his forepaw out with a big thorn stuck in it. You just have to drop everything and take it out before you move onto the grooming and training. This thorn in my patient got stuck in high-school and hasn't come out on its own. That was over twenty years ago. He has never completely let go of her. She did the right thing by dumping him. His energy is possessive, domineering, and selfish. He got dumped twenty years ago and still feels like he has a right to be here. I doubt it is conscious on his part; it's just the nature of his mismanaged energy. He sinks his hooks in and never lets go, moving on from one lover to the next, setting his hooks, and never letting them go. He is like a big wad of gum; everything he touches, he bounces off of, leaving a sticky, elastic string that binds the last object to him, putting a drag on the energy systems of all persons involved, including his own. He is not my client – Jodie is – so my job is to remove his energy attachment from her system. He'll have to sort himself out when he is ready.

The first thing I have to do is to isolate the ex-boyfriend's energy and separate it from hers. This energy pattern feels like only an unpleasant lump to start with, but, as I investigate further, I can define it: male, selfish, domineering, possessive. I've got him!

"Can you say the first name of your ex-boyfriend please?" I've worked with her before a few times, and she's been through this drill before, but with other relationships, mostly family.

"Mark?" No response.

"No, not him."
"Andy?" Nothing.
"Not him either."
"Jeff?" Bingo!
"That's it. I've got him."
"You're kidding. That was like, twenty years ago." "Ah, yes. Some people just never let go."

"Ooh, it makes me feel all creepy!"

"Yeah, I know, it's kind of weird, but not uncommon at all. Lot's of people have these kinds of attachments. In fact, I think everybody does to some extent, but it's always good to get rid of them when we find them."

"Ooh, yes, get him out of me!"

"No problem. He's going to be easy," I assure her. I don't know how I know this, but I do. I can tell that his energy hook is not very strong. He is not in deeply. "He's been here a long time, but not for much longer."

"Good!" she exclaims.

It's much easier to remove him once he has been positively identified. I still haven't figured out why this is, but as soon as she says his name, I can feel his grip loosening. The first step to solving a problem is identifying it, right? I continue to sequester his energy until I feel confident that he's all bundled up, and then I begin to lift him out of Jodie.

"OK, I'm going to lift him out now."

I let my energy sink below his, so I can get underneath him, and then gently and slowly lift him out. It takes about ten minutes to do the whole procedure. I get him out of her energy field, move him out a safe distance, and then let him go. This one is simple. I don't have to worry about him attaching to someone else. His energy hook was specifically for Jodie; now that the hook has been separated from her, it will dissipate without the benefit of her unwittingly feeding the attachment with her own personal energy.

"Is he gone?" She asks.

"Yes, just this second I moved him on."

"I could feel it, like something yucky just left. Ooh, gross! I can't believe he's been in me all this time."

"Well, it's not quite 'him.' It's more like, just part of him was still holding on."

"I'm glad it's gone. Ugh."

I laugh.

We have to go through similar attachments, mostly family and coworkers, before I can get back to the big one. The big blockage isn't a spiritual attachment like the others; it's an emotional blockage. The main difference here is that this energy belongs to Jodie. She made it herself, probably with the help of another person at some point in her history, but, nevertheless, the energetic signature on this blockage is her own. I'm glad we've got a two-hour session, because this is going to take a while. This blockage is big and deep, and it's been here a long time.

Working at a distance is giving me a clarity that I haven't had before, like washing a dirty windshield. Suddenly a lot more detail comes through and you can see things coming from farther away. I begin my usual process of capturing the energy blockage, so I can bundle it up and take it out. This blockage is her anger. It's not all of her anger, or her ability to generate anger; it's a specific type of anger. It's unprocessed anger. It's anger that she felt at some point in her past, but was never able to completely get it out of her system, so it stayed inside and festered.

This isn't psychology; it's energy. It's stuck inside her and it's blocking her from progressing on some level of her being. If I can remove it, then she will be able, with some effort and perseverance, to get past her anger issues. If the blockage stays then it will be very difficult for her to continue to make personal growth because it will sabotage her efforts. Every time this tangled mass of anger finds an excuse to lash out, it will – leaving Jodie at the whim of her own unresolved emotional energy. A similar emotional blockage might form in the other person involved in the interaction, who will then carry it to the next one and so on, until Jodie's one original blockage is propagated a thousand times. This is why it is so important to resolve this type of energetic blockage whenever possible. When blockages are deep, like this one, the only way to resolve them is to follow them all the way back to their roots.

Now that I've got the energy of the emotional blockage isolated, I can begin to lift it out. Not only is it dense and heavy, it is also festering and enraged. It takes a lot of my energy to lift it. As I get the blockage to move, I can see that I haven't isolated it completely. There remains a strong column of energy penetrating deeply into Jodie's system. It is like a thick root; if I break it off here and remove the blockage, it will only grow back.

Usually the origin of a blockage goes back in time as it goes deeper into the energetic system. I stay with the unpleasant blockage, keeping it isolated from other energies, as I follow it back in time, deeper and deeper into Jodie's energetic system. With a blockage this deep, I would expect it to be from early childhood – a traumatic event, a change in family structure, or perhaps a sexual molestation. I get a sense that we are quickly moving backwards through time. We slip easily through her twenties. As we go back, I can tell there have been multiple instances of this energy coming up in her life experience and causing problems with relationships, but the root goes deeper.

The blockage flares on back into adolescence with multiple problems arising from it, but goes deeper still. As we continue farther back in time, nearer to her early childhood, the blockage of energy and emotion intensifies and condenses. I feel as if my whole body is being squeezed as we continue going back. The energy has become so intense and concentrated that I know I must be very close to the root issue. My cheeks are tingling and I feel like my body is being crushed. Just when I think we are getting to the root, something unexpected happens. The energy starts moving faster backwards in time, and I feel like I am getting sucked through a funnel. Everything is moving so fast, I can't keep track of it. It gets darker and denser as I'm propelled faster and faster. I have to use all of my energy and intention to stay with the increasing speed and intensity of the blockage as we get sucked down through the funnel.

Heartbeats pound in my ears as the tightening funnel squeezes out all light into darkness. I feel a sense of losing consciousness as I slip through the tightest point of the funnel. All at once my body gasps and takes in a huge breath. It feels like a sudden pressure has been released from inside and the resulting vacuum sucks in the outside air. At the same time, a blinding light and a sense of expansiveness comes to my senses. I am still with Jodie's energy, but her blockage has disappeared. She feels free and light, but I have the sense that we have not solved the problem. So I start to investigate this new territory, which is in a different place and time that seems like a rural setting somewhere in Europe. There is fear in the air – not Jodie's, just a general sense of fear. I can see a barn and cows, or, rather, I can sense them.

The setting starts to unfold – we are in the First World War. Jodie is in her twenties in her previous lifetime – before the onset of the emotional blockage, before the anger seized her. The men of the farm are away at war. Only Jodie is left, to tend the animals and care for the family farm. She is alone. Foreign soldiers happen onto the farm during their patrols and find her in the barn. She is young and beautiful. They are away from their commanding officers. They face death every day. They have killed other men. Their hearts are hardened by war and morality has been stripped from them. They seize Jodie and take from her the only things she has been able to hold onto for herself during these difficult times – her innocence, her dignity, and her composure. After the ravaging she is left with only fear, anger, and hostility. The foreign soldiers leave her, broken and dispirited, to continue her lonely life of toil. Her life ends shortly thereafter by means that I am not privy to, but the real damage has already been done. She carried this emotional trauma through to the end of her previous lifetime and on into the next one, her current lifetime. It has made Jodie's early life difficult for her and for her parents, it has ruined her relationships, and it has held her back from progressing spiritually. The emotional trauma carried over from her previous lifetime had become so much a part of her that Jodie accepted it as part of herself, but it isn't. It is merely a blockage caused by a severe trauma that insinuated itself into the fabric of her spiritual material and was carried into this lifetime when she was born. It will continue to cause problems and may even be carried into her next lifetime unless there is some intervention.

I take her energy back to the moment of the original trauma and hold it there. It is difficult to hold, but I cannot let it get away. This is where we have to do our work. It is in this terrifying area, at the root of her trauma, where the work needs to be done. In the meantime, I am still in contact with today's Jodie over the internet telephone. I explain everything to her. She recognizes how her anger has ruined relationships in her life. It has damaged her relationship with her daughter and is now threatening her second marriage. She has tried to change it with therapy and self-help techniques, but the anger always returns within familiar patterns. She is ready to be free of this trauma.

166

I ask Jodie to focus her mind on letting go. Usually I can do the work on my own, but this is complex, and I feel like I need all the help I can get. As Jodie begins to focus her mind, I can sense a change in the blockage. It instantly feels possible to remove this deep-rooted obstruction, but it is complicated.

I feel the energy of the foreign soldiers – not their malicious energy, but rather their pain, their anguish, and terrible sadness. They still suffer from their actions not only from the trauma they have caused but also from the trauma they have experienced. I see tunnels of energy, like elongated tubes of dull light, which have sprouted out from their wartime experiences and connect the trauma of the past to their current lifetimes. It is a huge spiderweb of interconnected suffering. I still see the energy tunnel sprouting from Jodie's original past life trauma into her present-day life. This is the tunnel we followed backwards through time to get to the root of the problem. The tunnel has grown branches that connect to her daughter and to her ex-husband, and from them to other people seemingly unrelated to her. I can see it all at once, everything at the same time. The consequences of this trauma are too much for me to fully consider at the moment, but it is clear that I must do everything I can to remove this blockage at its source. Like a weed pulled out by the root, its branches of despair will wither and die, and eventually compost into fertile soil.

My whole body is sweating as I work to resolve the matter before me. Ninety minutes into the session I begin to lift this massive blockage from her, but it is too heavy and dense. Unable to lift it on my own, I stop trying. Instead, I put forth my energy to contain it, and I concentrate on opening myself to outside help. Within seconds, I see a door opening from some distant place, and a bright light spills through. The light beams like a column from the door down to the Jodie of the past. I feel a joyful sensation as this higher spiritual energy connects both to mine and to Jodie's energy systems. I can hear her begin to sob on the other end of the telephone line. I let go of my personal intention, and instead concentrate on facilitating the work of this higher spiritual light that has come down to help. The more I relax, the easier it is for this higher spirit to work. I can see the dense, heavy, dark, emotional blockage lifting out of Jodie. Other light doors open and connect to the energy of the foreign soldiers, who suddenly disappear like little light bulbs winking out. Jodie's blockage is being lifted out of her previous body in her previous lifetime. My energy and the energy of Jodie's blockage are now being moved forward through the tunnel of time. I can feel myself being squeezed through the funnel of her lifetime portal that opens into her current lifetime. We continue to move forward through her childhood, her young adulthood, her first marriage, and the birth of her daughter, and then onward into her current marriage and finally into her body as it is now. From here the blockage is removed up, up, and away. The higher spirit releases my energy and the light door closes. It's done.

I scan Jodie's energy for the blockage and no longer find it. I ask her how she feels. A melodious laugh comes from her as she says, "I don't know. Good. Strange. Lighter." With this blockage gone she can begin again to grow forward from where she left off in her previous lifetime. It's up to her, but with work she can move forward on her path free of the ball and chain of past emotional trauma.

Commentary from Spirit

Love connects us positively through channels of light weaving the web of humanity, then pain connects us adversely, binding us all in darkness. I am speaking of internal pain that is carried deep inside and continues without resolution.
So, do the work. Resolve your pain and free humanity from the bindings that you impose with your own suffering.
Free yourself to reconnect to the web of light.

The Soul Baby, the Trickster, and the Golden Buddha

Quote from Spirit

When the destination is reached, the pathway becomes irrelevant.

~William

Meditation is supposed to be a peaceful process of exploring the inner self. At least that's what I used to think. I have found that navigating the waves of inner turmoil in search of peace and enlightenment can lead you to new discoveries, but it can also land you on some rocky shores.

Living cheaply in Thailand with some money in the bank and no clinic schedule, I have the time to follow the unfolding of each meditative practice without the need to stop and get ready for morning clinic. If Five Finger Meditation takes five minutes or forty- five minutes, I follow it through to the end. My qigong, standing meditation, and sitting meditations are no longer framed by time. They have a beginning, middle, and end determined by the internal meditative journey, not by the clock. By practicing in this organic way, my meditations can better provide an avenue for the change that I feel is coming.

Each day's practice is becoming a revelation. I am finding and clearing blockages within myself, calming my mind, and purifying my energy. Today, sitting meditation and qigong are just a warm up for standing meditation – the Chinese call it zhan zhuang, "Standing Like Tree." It's a simple but very effective qigong practice for strengthening the body and maintaining health. There are many methods and ways of understanding zhan zhuang. For the moment, I don't use any of them. I simply stand and let whatever needs to happen, happen on it's own without my conscious guidance.

This morning's Five Finger Meditation made my emotions free and light, and sitting meditation has cleared my mind. So now, comfortable in my body and with a clear mind, I move into the Standing Like Tree meditation. I stand with both feet flat on the ground, shoulder-width apart, with my arms raised in front of me at chest-level forming a circle. Shoulders, hips and knees relaxed, head suspended. I take some moments to relax into my posture and let my body find its equilibrium. And then I simply stand and wait.

After twenty minutes in this posture, I am ready to end today's zhan zhuang practice. So I begin to draw in a long, slow breath, my final inhalation before exhaling and finishing the meditation. When my lungs are filled to capacity, I then begin a gentle exhalation, letting the air escape through my lips, not my nose. Without warning, halfway through the exhalation I am seized by a convulsive spasm. My body lurches forward and bends at the waist. The breath gets stuck in my throat and can only escape as a high-pitched wheeze. I feel my insides being ripped up at the bottom of my gut. I am being squeezed like a tube of toothpaste. In my mind's eye I see green bile pouring out the top of my head. Suddenly, every cell in my body is spewing forth its toxic waste into the stream of bile. It's like I am throwing up, but the volume of the green bile energy vomit is more than my entire body can carry. It is coming from unseen dimensions of my being. And it keeps coming. Gallons and gallons, a boatload of bile from my nonphysical being is rushing to find its way out through the top of my head. Physically, I am bent over and retching, fighting to catch my breath. Emotionally, I am dissociated, watching this event occur from a spot near, but not in my body. The onslaught of green energy bile continues without remorse. My legs quiver. My body shakes. I sweat. With legs trembling, I am barely able to remain standing when the last of the noxious bile finds its way out of my system leaving me lighter, emptier, purer.

I straighten up my body and try to recover my breath. Three feet in front of me, in the wake of the bile trail, I see a form. It is semi-translucent, floating in mid-air, capturing my complete attention: it is an embryo. It begins to grow before my eyes, slowly, from an embryo to the size of a baby. As a baby, it draws nearer to me. I take it into my arms. Then it grows to the size of a small child. As it continues to grow, I put it down. It stands on it's own, facing me; then it grows into a young man. It is me. We stand facing each other for a few seconds, then the young man walks into my body. Into me. It is me and I am it.

A million micro-adjustments begin to occur in my body. I feel the tiniest muscle fibers quiver and spasm; spontaneous posture adjustments realign my hips, shoulders, neck and head. I want to laugh. I want to cry. I want to jump up and down and yell from the rooftops. I want to go into solitude. But before I can do anything, something else happens. In front of me, small door in space, just to the right of center, begins to slowly open into blackness, and then it is pushed open by a surge of force. I feel the whole front right side of my body splitting open like a burst seam, and from the opening in my body spews out black bile. As happened with the green bile, the quantity is more than I could possibly hold in my small body. A truckload of black energy bile is pouring out from my deeper self. How could I have held so much toxic sludge inside of me? I am being emptied ten times over by the unyielding rush of poisonous black bile, spewing out with the force of a bursting damn. Ten minutes go by, and still it keeps gushing. Finally, it ends. The door shuts.

Standing next to the closed door is a small man whose image is too vague to recognize. At the same moment, in the air near my right shoulder, a golden Buddha floats. He is clearly visible – sitting, smiling, and radiating a brilliant golden luminescence. At this moment my mind opens to a new form of communication. Someone begins talking to me. The voice is coming from far above.

"Hear us and speak our words so that we may speak through you. We are here for your benefit and for the benefit of others. Our message is love."

Is the voice talking to me? The Buddha still shines in the air. The little man scoffs at the voice and pushes the door open again. It opens into blackness, but this time I can see into the darkness. It is reverse light. The darker it is, the brighter it seems. Clearly visible in the blackness is a form like the visual representations of a black hole, a funnel shape, wide on top and infinitesimally small at the bottom. What's at the bottom? I wonder. In a voice that is enticing, almost seductive, the little man says, "Infinite power." He offers it to me. All I have to do is walk through the black door. All the answers are there. Everything I could ever want or desire could be mine. It would be easy. But I hesitate. I want to go, but there is something wrong. I refuse the offer. A brilliant flash of white light explodes from the bottom of the black hole. Both the black hole and the little man vaporize. I feel a burst of anger, disgust, and outrage coming from the blast; the force is strong enough to physically knock me back several inches. The golden Buddha still smiles, but the little man is gone.

As I recover from the explosion, a brilliant white light appears in front of me. The little man materializes again, standing next to the white light. I realize who he is. He was in my clinic. He's the man who was helped by the angel-like being. He smiles and laughs at my sudden recognition of him. Gesturing with his hands, he bids me to indulge in the light. What is it – is it God?

"It's beyond God," answers Joe Cortez with a smile.

I want to go into this brilliant light. I am pulled toward it, but again something seems wrong. How can he show me something greater than God? I simply don't believe him. With this thought a shower of bright light begins to cascade down upon all of us from directly above. Joe Cortez, the doorway, everything is washed away by the light pouring down from above. The golden Buddha smiles and expands into the scintillating light. Everything is consumed completely by the light. I stand in light. I become the light.

I am Light.

Commentary from Spirit

Recognize your Self within yourself. Find the you who is on your spiritual path. Learn to live with, laugh with and finally let go of the ego persona you have carried for so long. It is the weight of illusion, the the stone around your neck keeping your head bent down in toil and struggle that keeps your eyes averted from the truth that awaits you.

Your ascendence is written. It cannot be avoided. Your path is lit, but you cannot see it. When your eyes open, the road to ascendence becomes wide and smooth. With your eyes closed, it is narrow, difficult, and strewn with stones. While your destination remains the same and your arrival ensured, you have the choice to trudge through unending lifetimes of misery and suffering or to travel with ease and grace on your journey.

To find your doorway to light, release your mind from its confines. Open your heart to the great web of love that connects all souls and join the harmony in which the universe sings.

Did you like this book?

Please write a review on Amazon.com Search: Michael Roland
Soul Baby Buddha

Attend a Retreat, Seminar, or get online training or work directly
with the author by becoming a FREE member of Circle of Light at
www.MichaelRoland.com

About the Author

Michael worked as an acupuncturist and doctor of Chinese
medicine for fifteen years. During that time he was in private
practice, taught at acupuncture schools and worked with the
prestigious Program in Integrative Medicine at the University of
Arizona. Currently, he consults remotely with private clients via
telephone, writes, and leads retreats and seminars worldwide.

CPSIA information can be obtained at www.ICGtesting.com
Printed in the USA
LVOW11s1936140715

446206LV00004B/417/P